Uncomplicated

Uncomplicated

SIMPLE SECRETS FOR
A COMPELLING LIFE

Brenda L. Yoder

Herald
PRESS

Harrisonburg, Virginia

Herald Press
PO Box 866, Harrisonburg, Virginia 22803
www.HeraldPress.com

Library of Congress Cataloging-in-Publication Data
Names: Yoder, Brenda L., author.
Title: Uncomplicated : simple secrets for a compelling life / Brenda L.
  Yoder.
Description: Harrisonburg, Virginia : Herald Press, [2024] | Includes
  bibliographical references.
Identifiers: LCCN 2023046337 (print) | LCCN 2023046338 (ebook) | ISBN
  9781513813028 (paperback) | ISBN 9781513813035 (hardcover) | ISBN
  9781513813042 (ebook)
Subjects: LCSH: Simplicity--Religious life--Christianity. | BISAC: RELIGION
  / Christian Living / Spiritual Growth | RELIGION / Christianity /
  Mennonite
Classification: LCC BJ1496 .Y59 2024 (print) | LCC BJ1496 (ebook) | DDC
  248.4--dc23/eng/20231214
LC record available at https://lccn.loc.gov/2023046337
LC ebook record available at https://lccn.loc.gov/2023046338

Study guides are available for many Herald Press titles at www.HeraldPress.com.

UNCOMPLICATED
© 2024 by Herald Press, Harrisonburg, Virginia 22803. 800-245-7894. All rights reserved.
Library of Congress Control Number: 2023046337
International Standard Book Number: 978-1-5138-1302-8 (paperback);
    978-1-5138-1303-5 (hardcover); 978-1-5138-1304-2 (ebook)
Printed in United States of America

Scripture quotations, unless otherwise noted, are taken from the *Holy Bible, New International Version*®, NIV®. Copyright © 1973, 1978, 1984, 2011 by Biblica, Inc.® Used by permission of Zondervan. All rights reserved worldwide. www.zondervan.com. The "NIV" and "New International Version" are trademarks registered in the United States Patent and Trademark Office by Biblica, Inc.® Scripture quotations marked (NKJV) taken from the *New King James Version*®. Copyright © 1982 by Thomas Nelson, Inc. Used by permission. All rights reserved. Scripture quotations marked (NLT) are taken from the *Holy Bible, New Living Translation*, copyright © 1996, 2004, 2015 by Tyndale House Foundation. Used by permission of Tyndale House Publishers, Inc., Carol Stream, Illinois 60188. All rights reserved. Scripture quotations marked (AMP) taken from the *Amplified® Bible*, Copyright © 2015 by The Lockman Foundation. Used by permission. www.lockman.org.

28 27 26 25 24   10 9 8 7 6 5 4 3 2 1

Contents

To the ordinary, compelling individuals who have imprinted my life and others in their circles of influence, including Naomi. And to Ron, for our beautiful life.

Foreword

While most of us would not want to give up the benefits of our modern life, many of us do sense that something is missing. We want to exchange chaos for peace. We desire to move from confusion to clarity. We long for connection, simplicity, peace, and real joy.

I recently spent a day going through photos with my eighty-five-year-old mother. As we looked through her photos, she shared her stories. Mom grow up in an era where hard work was valued, resourcefulness was necessary, humility was respected, prudence was needed, and loyalty was treasured. Her personal stories illustrated those character traits in a variety of ways.

The world has changed a lot in those eighty-five years. Certainly, there have been wonderful improvements that make our lives easier. We have washers and dryers, so we don't have to scrub our clothes in a washtub and hang them on a clothesline. We have indoor plumbing, so we don't have to go to the outhouse to use the bathroom. We have dishwashers that wash and sanitize our dishes, so we don't have to stand at the sink and scrub after each meal. We have reliable vehicles that get us from point A to point B with an automatic transmission that doesn't even require us to shift gears. Progress is wonderful in so many ways.

Yet there have also been losses that most of us have been unaware of. Character traits that are honed on the anvil of hard work, like perseverance, and wisdom that is passed on from one generation to the next are missing. While technology has seemingly simplified our life, it has also complicated relationships in so many ways. Sustainable rhythms of life that ground us to something bigger than ourselves are glaringly absent. Anxiety is on the rise, and mental health disorders are increasing.

To find the simplicity, peace, and contentment we are looking for, we have to value the technological advances while also embracing and cultivating timeless character traits that generations before us appreciated. We must lean into a faith that holds us steady. We desperately need a voice of reason in our lives, and Brenda L. Yoder is the perfect teacher for us.

As a wife and mother who lives on a farm in Amish country, Brenda has had a front row seat to the simple secrets for a compelling life that we long to know. Her experience as a licensed therapist adds to her wisdom on what's most important in life. Her work as an elementary school counselor gives witness to what happens in family units and in our personal lives when these timeless character traits are missing.

This book is full of the kind of hard-earned wisdom that's gleaned from women who have come before us. If you're looking for direction on how to live a meaningful, uncomplicated, and vibrant life, this is your book. Brenda will not only teach you how to live an uncomplicated life—she will give you practical next steps to make it happen. It's a book I think every woman should read, and I highly recommend it.

—Jill Savage
host of the *No More Perfect Podcast* and author
of *Living with Less So Your Family Has More*

Introduction

We find ourselves inwardly yearning for "that something" the Amish seem to possess with their lack, and which we lack; the serenity, the quietness, the sense of where you belong in a defined community.
—Kevin D. Miller, "What the Amish Can Teach Us"[1]

I know all about the town where you live. I read those Amish books," a sweet older woman said as she sat beside me at a speaking event. "Your last name is Yoder. Are you Amish?"

I hate disappointing people, but didn't she notice my high-heeled boots and sparkly jewelry? "I'm not Amish," I said, "but I am Mennonite!"

She smiled at this consolation prize I offered. I explained to her—as I do anyone who asks me about being Amish due to my last name and hometown—that I have electricity, drive a car, and go to a church like other "English" people. ("English" is a term used to identify non-Amish people in our local area). I told her I grew up in our town and that my husband and I had raised our kids on his family farm a few miles away.

Several other women sitting nearby said they love visiting our Amish and Mennonite community of Shipshewana,

Indiana, a popular Midwest tourist destination. We're known for our old-fashioned, simple ways, small-town charm, and well-cared-for farms. We've remained somewhat insulated and undeterred from the complicated goings-on of the outside world. People visit from all over. We seem to have *that something*.

Our lifestyle is one we "English" may take for granted. Having lived here most of my life, I'm not the only one who grew up presuming a compelling life was found elsewhere. Few things change here. When they do, it's gradual. Stores are closed on Sundays. The 7:30 a.m. coffee tables at local restaurants have the same customers who have been there for decades. And like the movie *Hoosiers,* we have a strong basketball tradition that carries us through the Midwest winter, often bringing home conference trophies and even a state title or two.

JUST LIKE YOU

Happenings in the broader world take a while to reach us. Two suburbia friends were visiting our area on their annual weekend when national events started to be canceled in March 2020. Supposedly a pandemic was upon us. I joked that they were safe in Shipshewana. "Those things 'out there' don't come here," I said, having lived in our more sheltered community since early childhood.

A few days later, our local schools closed.

As it did everywhere else, the pandemic affected our area. My father died from COVID-related complications. His death was among many heartbreaking losses that affected our small community.

Yet we shared in each other's grief. One woman delivered decorative signs at Christmas for families of COVID deaths.

A classmate delivered bags with gifts to grieving family members. A young mom made Thanksgiving dinners and delivered them to the new widows and widowers, including my mother. These ladies are just a few of the ordinary women leading uncomplicated, compelling lives by doing what they have seen modeled by their mothers and grandmothers.

Like many storms in life, it took the pandemic's chaos and loss to expose the rich, ordinary resources I took for granted. Perhaps you experienced something similar. Familiar rhythms sustained me during the early lockdown days. Spring planting started, just as it had for decades. The garden produce preserved in my basement lessened my anxieties when items were scarce. Hope was present as the sunrise and farm landscapes around us remained the same as they had for centuries.

Did you too notice the sunrise and sunset more or value the stillness and pause in our lives? Nature and God seemed to call us back to the basics of life and humanity. No matter where you lived, the sun rose with daily hope, and the night ended with a dependable rhythm that has sustained generations. This book attempts to connect with *that something* from the past that grounds us today.

FARM LIFE

A sign in our entryway says farming is a profession of hope.[2] It's true. I didn't grow up on a farm. My family lived in cities before moving to Shipshewana when I was three. Throughout high school, I dated Ron, a Mennonite farm kid I married. Our worlds could not have been more different. My dad was the son of Italian immigrants. Ron's family settled in the area with the first wave of Amish-Mennonite pioneers almost two hundred years ago. Our marriage resembles the movie *My Big Fat Greek Wedding*.

I knew little about farm life as a young bride. I thought potatoes came from a grocery store, not your garden. I quickly learned to preserve produce, making jams and sauces of all kinds. I learned to milk cows and bottle-feed calves while carrying a baby in a knapsack.

I'm also a professional woman. I was a stay-at-home mom for over a decade when our four kids were young; then I returned to teaching for several years before attending graduate school full-time to become a therapist and school counselor. I also write and speak.

Like you, my life is full. Ron taught secondary math for thirty-four years while managing a dairy herd for half of those. He retired recently from education and drives commercially for an Amish business. We often visit our adult kids and grandkids living out of the area and welcome them home when they return. We raise a menagerie of animals and host an Airbnb suite in our empty nest spaces.

You may say our life is busy, but Ron and I have more leisure time now than we did years ago when he milked cows. In our community, most people work hard, play hard, and rest on Sunday, just as we have for years.

WHAT ORDINARY FOLK KNOW

Even in a peaceful Amish country, life is hurried. You do what's most pressing, then move on to the next task. I've been in the counseling office one minute, milking a goat the next, speaking to hundreds in the afternoon, and nursing a baby animal at night.

Here, we employ folk knowledge—what ordinary people know through life experiences—while we adapt to newer technologies. This grounding knowledge informs us that complicated problems don't have to uproot your life, faith, or future.

You can face them head-on because no matter what happens or what sorrows you carry, children must be raised, crops must be harvested, and cows must be milked.

WHAT *UNCOMPLICATED* WILL TEACH YOU

Through conversations in the counseling office, with Airbnb guests, and with women across the country, I've learned people have a hunger and need for *that something* that has quickly evaporated from modern life. Visiting Amish country won't transfer the skills and values you long for to your life. But tools from *Uncomplicated* will.

I've written *Uncomplicated: Simple Secrets for a Compelling Life* for souls longing to sit at the table with those who have sustainable practices we hope to incorporate into our hectic, complicated lives. We want the wisdom of our grandmothers, the Amish, and the homestead lifestyle that intrigues us, but we don't want to give up the best of contemporary living. We also don't want the chaotic culture that accompanies modern life. Even if we have *that something* that the Amish or wiser forebearers had, how do we incorporate these old-fashioned virtues, mindsets, and behaviors into our lives?

I've wondered that too. The pandemic reminded me that *the something* I searched for most of my life existed in the natural processes and life God crafted. The same is true for you. We simply need to see a model of how to live the uncomplicated and vibrant life we hope for. With some simple secrets, we can launch our roots deep, planting ourselves in the present so that God can grow *that something* for future generations.

STORIES AND CIRCLES OF INFLUENCE

Some say the greatest textbook you can learn from is some-one's life. I agree. This book contains lessons, observations, and stories from many people whose lives compel me to be more like them. These influential people may not have books with their names on them, but their legacies are written in the hearts of hundreds of people who witnessed their lives.

It's unfair to romanticize any environment or lifestyle, whether of the country, of the past, or of the Amish and Mennonite faith cultures. I'm not a spokesperson for any of them, though they all shape my life. Because the faith traditions of my community value simplicity and humility, I have kept most of the stories to what I've learned from my own life and from other's lives. Many names in the book have been changed and situations modified.

Similarly, each chapter will invite you to identify someone who has impacted your life and models the chapter's mindset, behavior, or virtue. You will also be prompted to consider how your lessons and stories can similarly impact others in your spheres of influence.

I'll also refer to women from a book series called *Memories of Hoosier Homemakers*.[3] The series consists of interviews with Indiana homemakers who lived from the 1890s through the 1940s. These compelling women rose to life's challenges with resourcefulness, discernment, and hope, and they have greatly influenced my life.

SIMPLE SECRETS

Finally, the secrets in *Uncomplicated* correlate with essential life skills identified by the World Health Organization.[4] The virtues, mindsets, and behaviors here include contentment, prudence, resourcefulness, practicality, fidelity, forbearance and equanimity, stewardship, interdependence, groundedness and humility, and foresight (legacy and heritage). I could have included more, but that would complicate things.

I'm excited to share the richness of a life that doesn't change like shifting shadows. These virtues, mindsets, and behaviors are God's ways, seen in nature, humanity, and the Bible. Like you, I've learned many of them the hard way and am still mastering them. The attributes relate directly to your life, community, and home and are sustainable through life's advancements. Because just when you get life figured out, things change—even in Shipshewana.

THINGS CHANGE

Ron and I no longer milk goats; he and his family no longer milk cows, though his brothers still farm full-time. The milking parlor sits quiet and empty with the memories of a more hurried life. We and Ron's siblings live within a few yards of one another on the land where his parents built their lives. The farm's lessons, skills, and values are embedded here.

My little hometown continues to grow and change. Many popular entertainers have concerts here amidst our quaint shops. While these landscapes evolve, though, roots remain. The kind that won't uproot with each storm. Instead, it drives them deeper to anchor the trees that shelter and shade their environment.

So come with me as we learn simple secrets for a compelling life. You can wear chore boots or dress boots. They both get the job done.

Chapter 1

{CONTENTMENT}

A Beautiful Life

Contentment is the only real wealth.
—Alfred Nobel[1]

Mom, why do you always want to move?" my son asked as I was captivated by a big Victorian house we passed while driving. Since childhood, I've wanted to live in an old home, with whispers of an uncomplicated, simpler era when there was less pressure just to be. Such homes seem to have *that something* that connected with my soul as one who didn't feel like I belonged anywhere, especially in the present. When traveling through historical neighborhoods, I would often say, "That looks like a nice place to live," while imagining my life in that setting.

You can't hide anything from kids. Ethan knew we wouldn't live anywhere other than Shipshewana, Indiana. His dad managed the family dairy farm, and we'd recently built a new home across the road. But his comment revealed something I'd struggled with for years yet never spoke out loud.

Before we married, Ron's grandparents had asked us to live in their old farmhouse several miles from the farm. My "old soul" felt at home there with the big barn, summer kitchen, and smokehouse that seemed frozen in time. The giant shade trees welcomed me and told me they would shelter me from modern-day stresses. The generational homestead encompassed the past, present, and future, full of hopes and dreams, including a place where I belonged.

Then plans changed when Ron's grandmother died a few months later. Grandpa lived in his home for twenty more years until his death. Meanwhile, Ron and I went on with our life. We bought a little house outside of town, where we started our family and lived for the first decade of marriage. Ron took on more responsibilities managing the dairy herd, so we planned to build our permanent home near his family farm. Relinquishing the dream of living at Grandpa's was hard; it was like giving up *that something* I longed for in my life but couldn't name.

The local high school Building Trades program custom-built our modest modern farmhouse. We were practical in designing the home on a one-income budget, buying fixtures at auctions and scouting for the best toilet deals.

The home's features replicated the older ones I dreamed of before vintage and farmhouse styles were trendy. Décor included family antiques and garage sale treasures. I even scoured the area for an old outhouse to complete the old-timey look. Some women want diamonds. I wanted a one-holer.

Having a new home was nice, but I was restless. We weren't moving anywhere. That was the problem.

SOMEWHERE OUT THERE

Living in Amish country was not the life I dreamed of when I was growing up in Shipshewana. Almost half of our community's population drives horses and buggies. As a teen, I imagined myself as a journalist living in more compelling places like Chicago or New England. Staying in Nowhere, Indiana, was not on my bucket list.

But I fell in love with a Mennonite farmer and married the summer before I graduated from college. When I would visit my sorority friends on campus during my senior year, they would ask me what it was like to be married. I once told them I had canned 28 quarts of green beans over the weekend. Their awkward, silent response made it clear how much their contemporary lifestyle contrasted with mine.

I had my kids young and was a stay-at-home mom for over a decade. I was happy with our rural young family life. But as the years passed, I struggled with discontentment and doubt, searching for *that something* I didn't have. *What if* and *if only* questions make you believe the best life is not the one you are living.

Ethan's perception challenged me that day. He named an internal struggle I was ashamed to admit. Canning green beans, shopping at Walmart, and carpooling kids had lost their luster long ago. I often assumed God's best for me was different than my reality. Perhaps you've had these thoughts, too.

CONTENTMENT: THE FIRST SECRET

Contentment—the first secret to a compelling life—is *that something* humans have searched for since the garden of Eden. Our lack of it creates a sense that what we have or who we are just isn't enough. It makes us believe a satisfying life is always just beyond our reach. Like Eve in Genesis, I questioned whether the life God created for me could be all there was.

Contentment is a state of unconditional happiness or satisfaction no matter what you do or don't have. If you ask most people, they will say their life goals are to be happy or for their children to be happy. But happiness is misleading: you can be happy drinking your favorite coffee blend. Contentment runs deeper. It quenches an intrinsic longing for satisfaction with our lives and who we are.

Contentment was the first human struggle, which has complicated every human's life since creation. This is somewhat comforting—I'm not entirely alone as I let you in on my secret struggle with contentment. The good news is God knows about this struggle and lives here with us, just as he did with Adam and Eve.

At creation, God created a vibrant, satisfying life for the first humans as he does for us. He walked and talked intimately with them in a beautiful environment. What more could they want? But the seed of discontentment was planted by God's enemy when he whispered, "Did God really create his best for you? There's something over there that's better." Doubt and discontentment go hand in hand. They keep us searching for *that something* we think we're missing.

I've believed these lies. I wonder if you have, too.

SIMPLE HARMONY

While Ethan thought I wanted to move, I realized what I was searching for was a place to call home—where I could settle in, be myself, and belong. Moving into our homogenous Amish and Mennonite community as a young child, I knew early on that my family was different. In grade school, my Italian last name awkwardly contrasted with the Yoders and Millers surrounding me. I was taller than most girls. I was animated and talked too much. I felt like a bull in a china shop among my peers. If I were smaller, I thought, then perhaps I would finally fit in.

I started dieting at the end of seventh grade and didn't stop. Within a few months, I was eighty-eight pounds and diagnosed with anorexia nervosa. I eventually became bulimic. Control over food and weight was how I managed emotions and protected myself until my early twenties. Having an eating disorder defined me, and knowledge of it followed me in a community where everyone knew more than your name.

I started dating Ron shortly before I turned sixteen. Attending his rural Mennonite church for the first time, I was surprised that no one looked at me strangely or commented on how thin I was. People genuinely welcomed me. Though they lived just a few miles from my home, their lifestyle differed. Their plain building, without a steeple or stained-glass windows, made me curious about their uncomplicated ways.

During that first service I attended, a chorister asked us to open a worn old hymnal. He hummed a note from a pitch pipe, and the congregation responded by matching the pitch in a blended voice. I listened in wonder as they sang in perfect a cappella four-part harmony. After the sermon, the older pastor led the congregation in the chorus, "God is so good, he's so good to me." The assembly knew it by heart and sang it as if they meant it.

I felt at home there. I didn't feel pressure in Ron's faith culture or his family to strive, conform, or keep up with the outside world. Becoming part of a community content with God's goodness and a simpler life met a need deep inside me. I wonder if you have this need, too.

THE SECRET OF LIFE

What was different about Ron's faith community, an uncommon facet of Amish and Mennonite cultures, is that they value and practice simplicity and worldly separation as part of their historical tenets. Materialism and consumerism are generally seen as lifestyles to avoid. Not being raised with these values, I quickly embraced them, as they had those whispers of bygone eras. But it took longer for their beauty and worth to settle in my bones.

I was initially content as a thrifty, resourceful farm wife and stay-at-home mom. But I couldn't escape the lure of financial and material excess that permeated the broader culture of the 1990s and 2000s. I felt the social pressure to buy new. My garage sale finds grew less exciting than the newer, fancier things of others. Vintage wasn't trendy then—the words for it were *old* and *cheap*. The more I focused on the lifestyles of others, the more I believed the lie that my life was a less-than life and that *that something* could not be found there.

But by raising my kids in an environment where contentment is cultivated and practiced, I have learned its timeless value. The apostle Paul cited contentment as the secret of life: "I have learned the secret of being content in any and every situation, whether well fed or hungry, whether living in plenty or want. I can do all this through him who gives me strength" (Philippians 4:12–13).

NEEDS AND WANTS

Contentment feels both natural and unnatural to us. We witness this in toddler development. Young children seem satisfied by the simplest objects. They are curious explorers and play with whatever is within their reach to meet their instinctive need for play and enjoyment. It may be plastic lids or a large cardboard box.

But kids get easily distracted and bored as they receive toys with more dazzling features and experiences. Their desires change from needs to wants. We are similar. Better experiences and newer things squeeze out satisfaction with ordinary pleasures. It takes intentional practices not to succumb to materialism and worldly advancements. The discipline of distinguishing between needs and wants is a byproduct of past generations and modern farm life—a discipline I quickly learned as a young Mennonite farm wife.

On a farm, financial security is unpredictable due to weather, market prices, or unplanned disasters. Resources go into the machinery and next year's crop, not the latest kitchen gadgets. In general, you buy more of what you *need* than what you *want*. Similarly, earlier generations seem to have had a greater belief that quality of life, not material possessions, brought happiness. In the *Memories of Hoosier Homemakers* series, farmwife Bernice Esch sums this up well: "We've had a good life. There is nothing I want out there."[2]

This sentiment has finally become my own, though it has taken time. Bernice's secret of contentment and the apostle Paul's are available to you, too, even in your high-tech contemporary lifestyle. I've learned that it is all about perspective. Do you and I view our lives as half-empty, half-full, or full and overflowing cups?

HALF-EMPTY CUPS

At the time of Ethan's question, I faced the reality that I saw my life through a half-empty cup of discontentment. Why did I fail to see God's goodness? I had a beautiful house, a caring husband, and healthy, rambunctious kids. How could I be so restless and discontent? I asked myself what I was searching for and why.

I had to be honest. While it may have appeared to others that I had it all together, I still longed for acceptance and belonging. I no longer had disordered eating, but I pushed myself to be the ideal wife, mom, and community member to receive the respect of others I felt incapable of receiving otherwise. I yearned for a life without cultural pressures to fit in and to have it all together.

In God's grace, he doesn't condemn such struggles. Jesus understands the tension of not accepting the life God gives us. In another garden, the garden of Gethsemane, Jesus asked God to remove the cup he had been given. That cup encompassed all the disappointment, pain, and sorrow you and I may experience, even to death. Jesus identifies with our struggle in the most intimate places, especially in his moment of greatest human suffering.

When you and I wrestle with doubt, discontentment, or hopelessness from painful or hard circumstances, we can look to Jesus' words in John 18:11: "Shall I not drink the cup the Father has given me?" Jesus knew the human pain of experiencing circumstances that are not what we hoped for or expected. It's not natural for us to cultivate contentment in hardship or difficulty or when things don't seem to get better. Jesus felt this tension. He sits here with us.

God did not remove Jesus' cup, yet he found a way to accept it. You and I can cultivate a more contented life by embracing a different mindset based on gratitude to God, who sustains us, rather than focusing on our circumstances. This will turn our discontented or deeper heartache into a more palatable cup of acceptance, even if the circumstances don't change.

A NEW MINDSET

What can we learn from doubt and discontentment? Experiencing them can be a catalyst for growth and change. When they arise in you, be curious about their origin rather than letting your feelings dominate you. Restlessness may tell you something needs to change; you may be growing personally or professionally and may be ready for a new challenge or environment. Or the Holy Spirit may be prompting you to change a mindset, behavior, or lifestyle.

Such was the case when I read an email forwarded from a mentor during the pandemic. The lockdown created a new set of doubt and discontented feelings. Within the email newsletter was the question, "What if this life is as good as it gets?"[3] I looked outside my window on that 2020 spring day as I read it. I couldn't go anywhere. Instead, I went out on my porch, sat in a rocker, and watched the world around me while that question swirled in my head.

The grass before me was a vibrant green. White daffodils and purple hyacinths were blooming. The sun was a brighter yellow than I remembered. It was as if everything around me was in technicolor, bursting with breathtaking colors and beauty, like my personal garden of Eden. Wow, if *this life*, even in a lockdown, is as good it gets, then what God had given me was purely incredible!

The question, "What if this life is as good as it gets?" transformed what I had seen as a half-empty cup life into one that was full and overflowing. This reframed mindset continues to change me. Like Paul, you and I can be content—no matter our circumstances—by embracing the life he's allowed us to have.

It's challenging, though, to change our half-empty cup narrative. Our brains calibrate to negativity naturally. Rather than feeding discontented thoughts, train your mind to dwell on other things. Philippians 4:8 tells us to think about true, lovely, right, pure, noble, and admirable things. Memorize the scripture or write it down. When struggling with your thoughts, think through each attribute, thanking God and picturing those things in your full and overflowing life.

THE RIGHT VOICES

"You need to fill your mind with the right voices," I told someone who was struggling with a negative mindset. Messages all around us feed discontentment and doubt, especially on social media. "If only I had that, then things would be easier." "If only I looked like this, then. . ." Negative narratives are endless.

Doubts can also arise from faith messages that make it seem like God is more present or active in the lives of others. Social media postings about God's #blessings can make you feel like you're doing something wrong when your prayers go unanswered. God can seem far away. You may even question whether he cares.

There was a season when I experienced personal hurt and professional disappointments, one after another. Several prayers went unanswered. A half-empty cup perspective fostered doubt and discontentment, even about God. Could I trust him? God seemed close to others, but not to me. I was embarrassed to have such thoughts. I needed wise voices to ground my questions and speculation.

One day during this season, I was sorting through a storage box when a book piqued my interest. Its title was *Streams in the Desert,* which described my dry, desolate experience. An inscription on the inside cover said Ron's grandma, an old-fashioned Mennonite woman, received the book in 1964. Curious, I began reading the devotional, hoping it offered a different voice than what I heard from the shallow culture around me.

It did. The author, Lettie Cowman, spoke about similar feelings of restlessness, doubt, and discontentment. A missionary to Japan in the early 1900s, Mrs. Cowman wrote about God's goodness even in adversity. Her encouraging wisdom was the steady voice I longed for.

Romans 12:2 says we shouldn't conform to the world's patterns but be transformed by renewing our minds. The daily practice of reading *Streams in the Desert* started turning discontentment and doubt into contentment and trust. It has helped me see how rich and compelling life is, despite its trials, disappointments, and mundaneness. Filling your mind with the right voices is essential in transforming a dissatisfied life to be compelling and content.

SCRIPTURE APPLICATION

To help my struggling faith, I also read the Psalms in the New King James Version for a fresh perspective. One morning during the lockdown, I read Psalm 90. The words created vibrant images for me, just like nature did when sitting on my porch. I kept reading them repeatedly because they addressed the uncertainty I experienced being stuck in my home. I returned to them for several months. Several verses transformed my mind and heart from "I can't be happy until this is over" to "What if this is my best life?" The verses continue to change me.

Psalm 90:12 says, "So teach us to number our days, that we may gain a heart of wisdom." God challenged me during the lockdown to consider every day as valuable as the ones before when things were normal. These words promise that appreciating each day of our life grows wisdom, no matter what we experience.

Then, Psalm 90:14–15 instructed me that we are to rejoice and be glad *all* our days, even those in which God has afflicted us. I began immersing my mind daily with gratitude rather than dwelling on fear and discontentment until the pandemic ended. I continue to hold to this promise by practicing gratefulness for who God is, even in pain, discomfort, and loss.

Finally, Psalm 90:17 completely changed my thinking. It says, "Let the beauty of the LORD. . . be upon us." This invitation from God to let his beauty and grace rest on us, wherever we are, refocused my attention on the simple, radiant life God provides. It ultimately inspired this book. Fixing my mind on this truth, I can see God's goodness all over our lives, regardless of our days or where we live.

Though our corners of the world are different, each is lovely. None is better than another. The secret of contentment is finding pleasure in God's beauty that rests upon the life he crafted for you and me.

MAKE CONTENTMENT A LIFESTYLE

How can we make contentment a lifestyle when we are distracted by materialism, idealism, and consumerism? Let's look at some examples.

My friend Yvonne was raised in an affluent home where most things were handed to her. She often felt pressure in this lifestyle and wanted a different experience for her children. I watched how she and her husband created something different. They purchased an old home that needed remodeling and saved money by doing many of the projects themselves. Their children worked alongside them, learning from hands-on experiences. Her life was less stressful than her upbringing without all the distractions of buying the next popular thing.

Many wonder how less can be more. Less to worry about brings more time to enjoy what you have, whether it's material items or a way of life. Uncluttered homes, heads, and hearts fill up with security and belonging rather than the pressure to have, do, or be more.

This kind of "less" is what the Yoder farmhouse, where Ron grew up, was filled with. It was a single-story home with only six rooms and an eat-in kitchen. A busy farmwife, Ron's mom raised four sons and had an open-door policy for grandkids, neighbors, and friends. You didn't notice the lack of fancy furnishings. Instead, you felt *that something* you can't put words to. Lois's well-worn furniture was welcoming and comfortable. Her small kitchen table was where you knew you belonged.

Many of us try to create a feeling of satisfaction and acceptance with picture-perfect décor, outward appearances, or a stellar résumé. Contentment, on the other hand, is a deeper, inward condition of the heart. In the *Memories of Hoosier Homemakers* series, Wanda Couch said consideration for others, sharing, and caring is what makes people happy.[4] Such a simple secret for a compelling life, even today. When we spend time with others or think about the needs of others, we're relieved of the burden to ruminate about our own needs and wants.

There's a saying that people remember you because of how you made them feel. Uncomplicating your life may be as simple as living out the discipline of gratitude for what you have rather than scrolling, searching for, and fixating on what you don't have. You don't need *more* or *better* to have a home or presence where others feel loved and cared for. It's something you can create without spending a dime.

LET GO OF EXPECTATIONS

Discontentment isn't solely attached to belongings or experiences; it also affects relationships. You may look to your spouse, children, friends, or parents to make you happy and satisfied. Unmet expectations are known to be the killer of good relationships.

Are you critical or discontent when others don't meet your desires? I've been guilty of this. It happens when we expect others to meet our needs rather than God. We compare or romanticize our relationships. Social media tells us our marriage is not good enough and our kids are not happy enough. It informs us of many messages we carry around in our half-empty cup.

I realized social media fed a half-empty cup perspective as a new empty-nest mom. I envied families with everyone home who posted about their full lives. Mine felt empty and sad. Many friends were no longer in my life because our paths didn't cross anymore. I also expected Ron to make me content like my kids did.

I needed to let go of these unmet expectations. I started by refraining from social media in the mornings until I prayed and studied the Bible. I deleted some apps. Rather than being discontent with the lack of friendships in my life, I connected weekly with at least one person whose relationship I valued, whether in person or through a text.

You may have similar feelings of discontentment in relationships, about yourself, or your life stage. What is one thing you can do to foster contentment? Some suggestions at the end of the chapter may help you cultivate more gentle, realistic expectations.

It's also important to reflect on how social media affects your happiness. Do you reach for your phone when you're unhappy or disappointed, looking for affirmative comments or likes? Do you compare your posts to others or post something with the intention to make you feel happy?

Above all, pray about your needs, expectations, and disappointments. Consider God's truth in Philippians 4:19, which says God will supply all your needs according to his glorious riches in Christ Jesus. Let the Holy Spirit, through Scripture, reveal how God may be drawing you to him rather than to others for your needs.

CULTIVATE CONTENTMENT

There are many ways to cultivate contentment at home, with relationships, or with yourself. Consider which area you'd like to nurture first. I'll share a few examples.

Beautiful spaces make me feel content. For cost-free pleasures, I may rearrange a room for a fresh look or create feelings of belonging and warmth with the soft glow of lamps or inexpensive throw pillows. These simple things buffer life's more complicated stresses.

Ron and I also try to foster contentment in our marriage. When we first wed, the older pastor from Ron's church told us his marriage secret. He and his wife often squeezed each other's hands three times in a row. It meant "I love you." My friends Jill and Mark Savage advise couples through their marriage retreats to always hold hands during prayer. Ron and I practice these powerful gestures that make us feel connected.

My friend Elizabeth shares another example. A city girl, she met and married a local man while in college. They moved back to his childhood farm and raised their children there. She says she's learned contentment from doing things with her husband around the farm. Chores don't seem like work to her because of the companionship of doing them together.

Past generations did simple things together more often, with the people closest to them. You don't have to be married or have a romantic partner to have this contentment. It comes from finding *that something* in your life—where you are, as you are—that brings you joy and belonging. That may be companionship with your pet, God, or nature. It maybe your job or hobby. Contentment comes from doing or being in the presence of who or what you love and appreciate. Let's look at some steps to incorporate contentment in your life.

SIMPLE SECRETS: NEXT STEPS

Now it's your turn. Here are simple suggestions to foster contentment and uncomplicate your life:

- Saturate yourself in gratitude. Focus on the beautiful things God supplies you rather than what you lack. Keep a gratitude journal or daily list.
- Recite your blessings for two minutes while on your daily commute, washing dishes, or sitting in the carpool line.
- Plan one daily activity you look forward to—reading a new novel, getting ice cream on the way home from work, or drinking coffee on your patio.
- Listen to podcasts or follow influencers who encourage you with positive messages. (Join me for the *Life Beyond the Picket Fence* or *Midlife Moms* podcast).
- Fill your physical spaces with simple pleasures. It may be a small flower arrangement, a stack of Post-it notes, or vintage books.
- Journal your feelings of discontentment. Give your thoughts and emotions to God, asking him to meet your needs.
- Identify unmet expectations that may be hindering contentment. Talk with someone who can help you reframe more realistic expectations.
- Do more of what brings you joy—painting, reading, listening to music, playing board games with your kids, or starting a new hobby.
- Accept what you can't change. Instead of longing for something different, look at God's beauty in your life.

Prayer pause: *Invite Jesus to reveal what he desires for you from this chapter.*

REFLECTION

1. In what areas do you struggle with discontentment (self, relationship, home, or season of life)? Be curious about why you struggle. Then take one step to grow in that area.

2. Who in your life exemplifies contentment? How would you like to emulate them?

3. What did you learn or what reflects your needs and hopes in this chapter? How will you apply that to your life?

4. What is one lesson of contentment you can retell to another person?

Chapter 2

Cows Must Be Milked

Do the next thing.
—**Elisabeth Elliot**[1]

I stood in the farmhouse breezeway on a gray, rainy day, listening to the hustle and bustle of emergency plans being put into action. A tornado had just ripped through the area, taking the roof off a neighbor's milking parlor a mile from the farm. The damage made the facilities nonoperational. Our neighbor desperately needed to get more than one hundred cows milked or risk significant losses, including his herd's health.

Our facilities were untouched by the winds. After much discussion between Ron's dad and his brothers, they quickly offered our parlor to milk the neighbor's cows. They would figure the other things out later; milk storage and pickup, where the extra cows would sleep, and feeding an additional one hundred cows while keeping the herds separate.

Right now, the cows had to be milked.

Ron, his brothers, and other neighbors got their pickup trucks, hooked cattle trailers behind them, and brought cows from the neighbor's farm to ours. Over the next few weeks, we adjusted our twice-a-day milking time to accommodate the additional herd. We made room for them to pasture and stay clean. I watched in amazement as those involved used creative problem-solving and efficiency to remedy a problematic situation.

This experience and many others like it impacted me as a dairy farmer's wife. Because no matter what obstacles you face, dairy cows must be milked twice a day, every day. The job is irrespective of your mood, holidays, health, or natural disasters. You must find a solution and make something work when disruptions or unplanned emergencies occur. There is no quitting or letting someone else solve the problem.

Ron milked cows with his brothers and parents all his life. For the first half of our marriage, he helped manage the family dairy farm in addition to teaching. It was a new lifestyle for a town girl like me. It required flexibility and resourcefulness I lacked growing up in a more structured environment. Farm life doesn't have office hours. Ron often worked long days because a machine broke, a cow got sick, or something took longer than usual. He always stayed and completed a job, no matter how hungry or tired he was.

You may call it grit or the ability to get something done. No matter what it looks like, it's *that something* skill we desperately need.

WHEN YOU DON'T KNOW WHAT TO DO

I was a young mom when I first heard Elisabeth Elliot's story. In 1956, she found herself a widow with a baby girl in the jungles of Ecuador after her missionary husband, Jim, was murdered by a group of indigenous Huaorani people. When asked how she handled the loss as a single mom living away from support, she responded with a phrase that shaped my life: You do the next thing.

Coping with disruptions, unplanned events, and crises was part of life's fabric in prior generations. Today, these things crush us. The expectation that life is good and that we deserve happiness robs us of our natural ability to problem-solve in difficult situations. Decades of seeking pleasure, leisure, and happiness have created a vacuum for responding to uncomfortable and unpleasant circumstances and feelings. When things are disappointing or hard, we focus on how life should be and how reality is not meeting our expectations.

The phrase *nothing is guaranteed* is more realistic. Revelation 21:4 says that only in heaven will there be no more death, mourning, crying, or pain. Hardships, disruptions, and problems don't need to overwhelm or overcome our ability to figure out solutions. God created us as problem-solving creatures. Our culture of comfort has weakened our healthy coping skills and replaced them with avoidance and anxiety. We're going to change that. Let's learn how resourcefulness can help.

RESOURCEFULNESS: THE SECOND SECRET

Resourcefulness—the second secret—is the ability and creativity to cope with difficult situations or unusual problems. I've used the "cows must be milked" analogy in the counseling office to illustrate that when complex or unexpected issues arise, we must use our available resources to determine the next steps. You and I can do hard things. We often must think outside of the box.

Resourceful people overcome challenging problems effectively and deal skillfully and promptly with new situations and difficulties. Farmers, medical professionals, managers, and educators are just a few who make such decisions routinely, fixing immediate problems and unexpected needs on the spot.

Such situations present themselves daily for me as I work with young children in an elementary school. I may try the best-researched strategies, but not all textbook answers meet a child's needs. Resourcefulness means attempting different solutions until a problem is solved.

Some days it feels like our current problems are so complicated that we simply can't solve them. They aren't. YouTube, Siri, and Google tell you how to fix almost anything except for those life problems that need human ingenuity. But we aren't the first generation to come up against difficult problems. Our grandparents didn't have YouTube or Google. Life was innately hard. They did the next thing until they figured things out and learned along the way. Giving up was not an option.

YOU CAN DO IT

When Ron and I first dated, I often visited the farm in the summer. I loved the energy there because something was always going on. One day, I visited with his mom in the kitchen when Ron's dad rushed in. They needed to get a small field of hay bailed before it rained. It was during milking time, so they were shorthanded. Bob asked me if I'd drive the tractor while he and Ron bailed. I thought he was joking. He was not.

On the farm, everyone helps to get the job done if needed. I knew nothing about driving a tractor. My only comparable experience was driving my dad's riding lawnmower.

I was ill-equipped but needed to be resourceful with the skills I knew. Like I did with lawn mowing, I tried to line up the tractor wheels on each row. I did my best to follow their directions as I carefully drove the tractor, worried that

I would crash. We finished bailing the field, but Bob teased me for years that it was the most crooked driving he had ever seen. The experience taught me that you *can* do things when needed, whether you think you can or not.

LIFE DOESN'T COME WITH INSTRUCTIONS

You are resourceful, too; you just don't know it. If you're a parent, you have practiced resourcefulness since bringing that baby home. Despite all the books and advice, nothing prepares you to care for your unique child. Children don't come with playbooks, and neither does life.

JoAnn Folke, a Hoosier Homemaker, reflected on how farm life had forced her to be resourceful: "Right after we married, I got pregnant. I was out on the farm, moved from town and knew nothing about farming. I was beside my mother-in-law when she died right after we married. I was just 19. I cooked for my husband and father-in-law and didn't know a thing. I cooked for three days for threshers, around 20 people that summer. I did it and didn't question it. Nobody asked me if I could do these things."[2]

You may find yourself in a situation you never planned for or imagined. If you haven't yet, life says you will. But there is always a way through. Dig into your skills and strengths, and creatively do the next thing.

YOUR RESOURCEFULNESS MAGIC

Before society turned toward a throw-away culture of convenience, households had less disposable income and "stuff." You fixed and reused things until they could no longer serve your needs. Then you discovered other uses for them.

We can look to our ancestors who lived during the Great Depression for lessons on ingenuity and know-how. When food was scarce, some mothers preserved dandelions or other edible weeds because they needed nutritious food for their families. We may balk when our pantry is empty, saying we "don't have food," but in our modern reality, we really mean that we don't have food that's convenient to eat quickly.

You may not want to serve weeds to your family or grow a garden. There are plenty of ways to adapt this principle to your specific lifestyle. Many in my community still employ the resourceful skills of growing gardens and preserving vegetables, though store-bought goods are readily available. My resourcefulness magic for years as a busy working mom of four growing kids was preserving garden produce and making multiple freezer meals. These were my meals of convenience.

Your resourcefulness magic is just as vital. What is it? You may meal plan or make homemade laundry soap for your child's allergies. You may know how to drive a stick-shift car or parallel park. Or you may know how to create an Excel sheet to track household expenses or organize a project at church. The lens of resourcefulness opens creative possibilities you cannot see at first glance, but which can help you and others thrive with determination and ingenuity.

YOU'LL FIGURE IT OUT

When teaching high schoolers about the Great Depression, I used a quilt top I purchased at an auction to explain the necessity of resourcefulness during that difficult era. The quilt top was made of tiny white squares cut from fabric feed sacks. It represented the untold story of a resourceful woman who used what she had to make a warm blanket for her family.

Many women used flour and feed sacks to make clothing during the 1930s and World War II. Manufacturers sold these bulk goods in fabric sacks with colorful prints that could be reused because viable resources were scarce. This quilt top was made from standard white muslin sacks, not the pretty prints. The blanket was a labor of utility, necessity, and love.

Resourcefulness helps us find working solutions for people we are responsible for, especially in adverse circumstances. Sometimes it's not something we do with our hands but with our hearts. When overwhelmed, a calm, steady response, letting the person know you'll figure things out, is better than false promises that everything will be okay. Resourceful people dig in and don't give up, especially when viable options are slim.

There is a slogan from the Depression era: "When you reach the end of your rope, tie a knot in it and hang on."[3] This can-do, we'll-make-it-work, authentic optimism is what our circles of influence need from us. It's a reality that compelled me to return to work in public schools during the pandemic. I was empowered to collaborate with others during a difficult time to create working solutions for kids so they could have in-person learning.

THERE'S AN APP FOR THAT

When the media first amplified messages of hopelessness during the pandemic, seeing my Amish neighbors' horses and buggies trot by gave me hope for working solutions. They reminded me that old processes, like the ones I grew up with, still worked and that I had the skills to get through such a difficult time. You do, too.

Think of resourcefulness and the other skills in *Uncomplicated* as an app on your phone. You have a wealth of skills you may only use occasionally. But you know how to use them when needed. You will not face a situation that God hasn't already prepared you for. All you need to do is tap into your brain and its experiences and creatively problem-solve. When facing an obstacle, tell yourself, "I have an app for that!" You'll be surprised when your human ingenuity is just what a situation needs.

Technology is great when it works, but when it doesn't, we often lose sight of its purpose—to get a more important job done. I've used a variety of technologies over my professional life, from chalkboards to iPads, and encountered issues with each one. At one speaking event, my computer had trouble syncing up with the projector. A few minutes turned to many as the audience waited. People grew restless. I finally asked if there was an overhead projector in the building. There was, packed away in a closet. With a flip of a switch on this forgotten technology, our workshop went on without interruptions.

Resourcefulness recognizes many ways to get a job done and knows how to improvise. Technology is just a tool, along with manual processes, though it's hard to remember this when we become reliant on the most high-tech solutions. You may feel differently, but when things go wrong, I want to be with someone who still uses a pen, paper, and their own two feet.

DON'T STEAL THE STRUGGLE

This practical know-how isn't just for emergencies or minor disruptions. Resourcefulness is a vital coping skill. Many don't know how to bridge the gap between problems and solutions because of various fears. Jonathan Haidt, co-author of *The Coddling of the American Mind*, says the more we strive for perfect safety, the harder it is to venture out into the world and learn its lessons.[4] I agree.

As educators, Ron and I observe increasing deficits in basic academic and life skills among students. We adults have stolen from them the art of human struggle. Removing academic, social, emotional, or relational challenges has caused an epidemic of enabling, entitlement, and lack of resourcefulness and healthy coping skills. Anxiety disorders have become the most common mental illness, affecting around 30 percent of all adults at some point in their lives.[5]

We find a powerful antidote to this epidemic in Scripture. Romans 5:3–4 says, "Suffering produces perseverance; perseverance, character; and character, hope." We build strength, resilience, and mental fortitude from perseverance and pain. Resourcefulness says you don't steal the lessons gained from persevering through a struggle. Instead, you lean into it and learn from it.

After living in a larger city for many years, our nephew and his wife moved back to Shipshewana. When I asked about the contrasts in environments, one difference Sophie mentioned was the pressure for kids to succeed at all costs in their former location. Here, she remarked, kids have the opportunity to fail. Doing so allows youth to grow and learn from mistakes in a safe environment while relieving the pressure parents experience among their peers if their kids don't excel.

A young adult recently told me that he embraces risk and failure. I was surprised and asked him why he felt that way. He said risks and failures teach you what to do differently the next time. Hoosier Homemaker Sarah Zeigler took it one step further, saying, "I don't think there is anything I can say that I failed in because you just keep trying, and if you keep trying, you don't really fail."[6] These perspectives encourage me to have a similar mindset.

You can help those in your circle of influence thrive by allowing a healthy amount of struggle, whether in your kids, grandkids, or yourself. Let natural problem-solving happen, whether in learning how to tie a shoe, recovering from a bad grade, or solving a relational issue. Fear of failure drives anxiety, avoidance, and feeling overwhelmed. Instead, let's create confidence by coaching ourselves and others to do hard things and learn from the process.

A NEW MINDSET

Survivors of the Holocaust or POW camps often report that they were able to survive by protecting the one resource they could control—their minds. Accepting the control we have over our feelings, responses, and behaviors makes problems more solvable. This also means accepting that we cannot change what is out of our control.

Resourcefulness means looking at what is within our reach to change. Resourceful people utilize knowledge and ingenuity and partner that with life experiences to recognize what is and is not within their control. They rely on God's strength to do within them what they can't do on their own, developing autonomy from circumstances rather than succumbing to victimization.

What does this mindset look like? Romans 12:2 tells us not to conform to the patterns of this world but to be transformed by renewing the mind. The patterns of today's world are worry, entitlement, ease, and helplessness. Renew your mind by accessing what you can control—your inner dialogue and the truth of God. Rather than saying you can't, believe you can figure something out, asking God to show you how. Instead of saying you don't know, say you'll find out. When you feel like something is too hard, tell yourself you can do hard things and that Christ's strength is made perfect in your weakness.

CELEBRATE YOUR SUCCESSES

God created your mind to analyze problems and think creatively for solutions. Each time you solve a problem, your brain develops a new pathway that says, "I figured this out!" It retrieves this memory and applies the experience when encountering new situations and challenges. When you have succeeded in one area, you'll believe you can leverage those skills in other areas.

We can encourage this by acknowledging when we or someone around us overcomes an obstacle. The Bible provides examples of celebrating milestone moments. Throughout the Old Testament, people built altars of worship for important events and created traditions and celebrations to remember what God brought them through. Similar practices are important for us.

How can you mark milestone moments? You may choose an object representing the event or celebrate it with a meal with someone. Or you may journal your growth. I try to reflect on that all-important question, "What did I learn?" However you do it, make a big deal when you or another person overcomes something. Today's hardships are tomorrow's stories that will impact others in ways you may never know.

BEAUTIFUL RESULTS

We have a creek behind our house that gets mucky and stagnant because the cows are fenced away and don't walk through the water to stir it up. They don't eat the green undergrowth, so the water flows slowly, and green algae forms on the top. Such an environment breeds mosquitos and other swampy things, which isn't desirable near our yard.

Looking at the green muck on top of the water, I knew the bottom of the creek needed to be dredged—a type of stirring up that would naturally be done by the cows. I figured if cows couldn't grate the bottom, I could to make the space beautiful again.

Ron was skeptical about my plan, but I was determined. Wearing my rubber rain boots, I cleaned the creek bed by walking back and forth with a metal garden rake digging the bottom of the creek bed. The green mess transformed into a clear creek bed with water that freely flowed. We now do the same process every spring. By midsummer, you can see the sand, stones, and shells on the bottom.

Resourcefulness often looks like a willingness to make something work. A mentor of mine, Janis Price, says that God will do what we can't. He will not do what we won't. Cleaning the creek bed is a visual analogy of a willingness to use available resources for the obstacles before us. Life is filled with muck and mire. Cleaning it out is messy and muddy. It often requires a less-than-pleasant effort. But when it's finished, it is clear, free, and beautiful.

SCRIPTURE APPLICATION

My creek bed determination exemplifies self-reliance, which has its place. But God really wants us to come to him with our problems. Philippians 4:6–7 says we should bring everything to God in prayer, and his peace, which passes all understanding, will guard our hearts and minds in Christ Jesus. I'll refer to this verse in later chapters because it's the most practical, specific application and promise we have regarding our needs.

God's resources are endless. Psalm 50:10 says everything belongs to God, including the cattle on a thousand hills. His provisions are not bound to financial or material possessions. They include skills, education, experiences, time, and community resources, to name a few. When we ask God to partner with us, resourcefulness expands to include his ways and wisdom, which are greater than what we can achieve on our own.

In *The Practice of the Presence of God*, Brother Lawrence, a seventeenth-century priest, prays, "Lord, I cannot do this unless you enable me."[7] This prayer is the opposite of self-reliance. It helps me recognize my frailties. It reminds me to come to God with my needs and receive his abundant resources. It helps me to see how God and I can tackle challenging situations.

A RESOURCEFUL LIFESTYLE

Resourcefulness means approaching what's in front of you and optimizing what you have, whether that involves making something new or thinking about how to do something better. In the professional world, it is a top "soft skill" linked to performance, development, and career success. Resourceful leaders are imaginative and persistent.

My niece is a New York City entrepreneur whose creative resourcefulness flows into all parts of life. She brightens her world by supporting small New York City businesses, shopping at farmer's markets, and lifting others up with her influence. She loves gardening and has created a rooftop garden atop her Manhattan apartment building to grow various flowers, vegetables, and even baby corn!

My coworker Annie is resourceful in other ways. Her degree in social work gives her a let's-figure-this-out outlook to solving problems for families in crisis. She is well-connected with community agencies and creatively problem-solves by connecting families with the right resources.

These women are people I look up to, along with several others in my community. They include people who are resourceful in difficult situations—caring for a terminally ill child, working two jobs, or safely handling a complicated relationship. You are one such person in the life of another. God is using your resourcefulness to encourage others to overcome the obstacles in their lives, too.

LET GO OF OBSTACLES

Resourceful problem-solving includes the ability to overcome big and small obstacles. Sometimes the obstacles are outside of ourselves, but often they are mindsets, behaviors, expectations, or responsibilities we must relinquish. It's easy to say, "I can't," and much more difficult to say, "I can, but it will be hard." Resourcefulness involves what we are willing to do, rather than the scope of the problem.

You may need to let go of a picture-perfect outcome and accept a solution that's not ideal but works. You may need to simplify your expectations. Often people only want to try the solution they desire and are unwilling to try other viable options. For example, a person may be stressed, with too many responsibilities, but be unwilling to delegate tasks; they aim for A-grade perfection rather than accepting that "C's get degrees." Instead, ask for help and be willing to learn. Create an "I'll figure this out, somehow" attitude with optimism and persistence to try different strategies until something works.

Another obstacle is information overload. Too many resources can often hurt rather than help situations. You may research how to do something and be overwhelmed by all you learn. Feeling flooded with choices, you fail to do anything. Next time, only look at a few options and try the one that looks best. If it doesn't work, then try another. Don't get stalled wondering what the perfect solution is.

For kids—and, let's be honest, for adults, too—hours of screen time are an obstacle to resourcefulness. Screen time hinders a child or teen's ability to focus, be creative, and manage emotions in the years these skills are being formed.

Children used to spend hours playing make-believe or creating new inventions. If you're raising kids, each hour spent with a screen takes away opportunities to develop strategic life skills. The same principles apply to adults, as screen time mutes the resourceful, creative skills we may have developed throughout our lives but are not consistently using.

Let's let go of obstacles and free up our creative energy!

CULTIVATE RESOURCEFULNESS

I recently worked with leaders on a project they had discussed implementing for years. They often got stuck because the obstacles seemed big. We worked together to identify the goal and obstacles. We brainstormed how to remove the barriers. We took one step at a time until we created the outcome they hoped for. The program was up and running sooner than anticipated.

Resourcefulness doesn't require such a formal process. Those cows needing to be milked were transported in a matter of hours. That creek bed just required a rake and a willingness to try. Once you learn resourcefulness, you naturally apply it to other areas of your life, from career changes to relationship struggles and creatively living on a budget.

I'd like to know what solutions your creative resourcefulness will find. It may be as small as fixing something broken, trying something new, facing an anxious situation, or solving an insurmountable financial problem. You have what it takes to figure it out, no matter what it is!

And you are not alone; God is with you. Ask him for wisdom and perseverance. Then do the next thing. Before you know it, you'll be known as one who can fix anything, both literally and figuratively. Your example of resourcefulness, ingenuity, and wisdom will help others find their resourcefulness magic, too.

SIMPLE SECRETS: NEXT STEPS

Now it's your turn. Here are simple suggestions to practice resourcefulness and uncomplicate your life.

- Be curious and ask questions when problems arise, such as "What else can I try?"
- Let your children try an activity or solve a problem before stepping in to help.
- Celebrate milestone moments in your life or family. Make a cake, buy a trinket, or start a family scrapbook to remember your milestone.
- Limit information when looking up questions online.
- Try your original ideas before looking for inspiration on Pinterest, YouTube, or other places.
- Learn a new skill you've been thinking about—using a power tool, baking with yeast, or creating an Excel sheet.
- Redo something with little or no cost.
- Try something new. If it works out, great! If not, that's an experience you learn from.
- Use your unique creativity when exploring options for solutions. How can your past experiences help you solve this problem?
- Practice identifying obstacles to problems or dilemmas.
- Don't be afraid to ask about various options. The worst that can happen is someone saying no. Someone might say yes, and a new door will be open.

Prayer pause: *Invite Jesus to reveal what he desires for you from this chapter.*

REFLECTION

1. What holds you back from being resourceful? What steps can you take to grow?
2. Who in your life exemplifies resourcefulness? How would you like to emulate them?
3. What is most helpful or what reflects your needs and hopes in this chapter? How will you apply that to your life?
4. What is one lesson of resourcefulness from your life that you can retell to another person?

Chapter 3

Press Pause

Prudence is the necessary ingredient in all the virtues, without which they degenerate into folly and excess.
—Jeremy Collier[1]

Ron walked to the barn for daily chores one fall morning before school. He has a routine of feeding the outdoor animals first before tending to the ones inside. This day, he did all the rounds before entering the barn to feed the goats and sheep.

We only had sheep for a few years, not long compared to the other animals we raised. Sheep are curious creatures, we have found. Beautiful and serene while grazing the pasture, but stubborn and ignorant otherwise.

Ron wasn't prepared for what he saw when he opened the barn door. Feed was strewn all over the cement floor, and a dead, bloated sheep was lying on its side. The sheep had jumped over the gate of its pen and got into a nearby fifty-pound feed bag. She had gorged herself to death without heeding the instinct of caution to tell her when to stop eating.

Ron came into the house and relayed the story, shaking his head, saying, "That sheep—she didn't know when to stop something that will hurt her." I listened to the story with shock and empathy. I recognized the qualities he described about the sheep within myself. I, too, had learned the hard way like her. How many times in my life had I not heeded caution and ended up hurting myself or doing something I regretted?

There's a reason sheep are used throughout the Bible as an example of human behavior. Without prudence, we get into a lot of trouble, which is probably why our culture is in a bit of a mess.

A LOST VIRTUE

Perhaps, like me, you have reaped the consequences of imprudence at some point in your life. Prudence was once considered the most valued virtue. It defined the character of the Greatest Generation who lived through the Great Depression and World War II. It is now shelved in museums of ancient relics alongside rotary phones and ration cards.

Pop culture tells us that if it feels good, do it, no matter the cost. That doesn't seem to be working well. American culture is a desert regarding sense and sensibility. Like the sheep, we often fail to pause and consider the consequences of our actions, whether it's our finances, health, relationships, or anything else.

Let's get this valuable virtue off the shelf and get it back to work.

PRUDENCE: THE THIRD SECRET

Prudence—the third secret—means discerning and measuring the consequences of an action, allowing you to avoid risks or dangers. It means pausing, acting moderately and cautiously, and respecting the life and freedom of others. Prudence is one of the four cardinal virtues which were originally identified by the philosophers Plato and Aristotle and have become part of the Catholic tradition.

Prudence is also highly valued by the Amish. In order to maintain their traditions, they must be cautious about how new technologies and advances affect their way of life. People looking at the Amish community from the outside may marvel at their ability to be unchanged by the broader culture. What we fail to consider is how deliberately the Amish must think about choices and behaviors. As one Amish woman said about how one action affects another, "Once you jump into one thing, then you jump into another."[2]

In an essay titled "Technological Prudence: What the Amish Can Teach Us," author Kevin D. Miller says the Amish prudently keep phones out of their homes, often a distance away in the neighborhood phone shack (as it is called in our community). The practice makes one consider the time and energy required to make a phone call and the need for the conversation. As Miller puts it, "If you have to walk a quarter of a mile to use the phone, you don't use it much."[3]

Would such discernment help our relationships and well-being? I think so. Developing prudence has helped me immensely to live free from disordered eating and reactive behaviors. This treasured virtue may have something important to teach us about more thoughtful and balanced living.

DRIVE IN THE MIDDLE LANE

One of my adult kids and I recently drove to O'Hare Airport in Chicago. Chicago driving is some of the worst in the country. Traffic jams happen at any time of day. Cars weave in and out of multiple lanes, often at high rates of speed.

My young adult is a seasoned driver, having lived in a large city, and offered to drive. Sitting beside him was a stretch for me as a mom. But I was pleasantly surprised. For most of the trip, he safely drove in the middle lane at a steady speed. I asked him why he didn't move to the faster outside lane. He responded that if you stayed in the middle lane, you reach your destination about the same time as you would racing back and forth in city traffic. You're also safer by minimizing the risks of missed exits or accidents.

The prudence of driving in the middle lane taught me something. It is a metaphor for cautious alertness and discretion most of us need in our lives. Many of us seem to lack this steady middle lane lifestyle, something I have noticed more frequently in people's mindsets and behaviors. I've recognized it within myself, particularly when I find myself surrounded by off-center thoughts fueled by fear or fatalism.

RISK MANAGEMENT

A few years ago, I needed professional advice about things outside of what I was familiar with. I shared my questions, concerns, and fears at dinner with a friend who was an expert in that field.

She leaned across the table and asked, "What's the worst that could happen?"

The question startled me. I was used to asking such questions as a therapist, not needing to be on the receiving end. I shared my worst fear. She wondered how I would handle things if my fears materialized. I imagined being in that scenario as we talked through various responses. My anxiety lessened. Our prudent conversation gave me the wisdom to mitigate risks.

Prudence helps us minimize danger and anticipate potential crises. The Amish consistently implement this kind of risk management in navigating the boundaries of their communal life. Acceptance of new technologies and lifestyle changes are ongoing negotiations around the Ordnung—the unwritten set of rules and guidelines for Amish church members. It is the governing parameter for lifestyle, morality, and business. Changes to the Ordnung are measured against the impact on the community, families, and beliefs.[4]

Most of us don't live in a community with such a clear set of boundaries and processes for exercising prudence. But what would it look like if we applied such discernment in avoiding risks and managing our relationships and resources well in our own lives? For examples of that, we can look to past generations who lived this well.

MONEY UNDER THE MATTRESS

My grandma came to the United States from Italy at the start of the Great Depression. Two babies had died in Sicily because her nutrition was so poor that she did not have enough breast milk. After she arrived in the United States, she had four more children, including my father.

Their family lived in tenement houses in various locations in Gary, Indiana. My grandfather worked in the steel mills, and Grandma was a prudent saver. For years, she stored money under a mattress for the down payment on a house, unbeknownst to my grandfather. That money allowed them to purchase a 668-square-foot home on two lots, which they proudly cared for until their deaths.

A prudent person plans and uses resources well. I'm inspired by how small steps bring us to a goal or dream, like meticulously saving to buy your first home. It's much more valuable than impulsively living on a whim because it safely takes us where we want to be, rather than creating unwanted or unforeseen consequences. What follows is a lighthearted example that taught me a great lesson about the dangers of imprudent decisions.

CARRIAGE RIDE IN THE MOONLIGHT

We had a pony one summer when the kids were young. Like our Amish neighbors, we also had a cart the pony pulled behind it. The kids drove the pony and cart around our property and down the lane at the family farm for fun, learning new skills and experiences with an unfamiliar animal.

When my sisters and their kids visited my parents that summer, I thought on a whim that driving the pony cart into town to show my nieces and nephew would be adventurous. It was a beautiful day, and the four-mile drive to Shipshewana would be gorgeous.

However, I had never driven something at four miles per hour. I was surprised at how late I arrived, realizing I needed to head home immediately to return before dark.

Not only did my lack of prudence cause longer-than-anticipated travel, but I hadn't considered that we lacked the legal reflective triangle required for carts or buggies on public roads. A police officer pulled me over about two miles from town at dusk to inform me of our safety violation. For safety's sake and caution, he turned on his flashing lights and followed behind my slow-moving vehicle the rest of the way home. I'm sure more than one motorist got their nightly entertainment from the English girl with the police escort clip-clopping in the moonlight.

RED FLAG FEELINGS

That's a humorous story about imprudence. But lack of caution and foolishness can truly have detrimental consequences, as modeled by the sheep and probably evidenced in many of our lives. It doesn't have to be that way. God innately equips us with healthy fear and its physical responses as alarms to potential harm. Prudence is our natural superpower, recognizing the importance of being alert and aware of danger.

As a counselor, I often help kids, teens, and adults to recognize the fight, flight, and freeze response they experience in unhealthy and unsafe situations. Prudence helps us to *pause* and listen to our body's red flags of caution. It may be recognizing rocky, wet terrain unsafe for you to walk on with your torn ACL. Or it may be listening to the voice telling you to abstain from one more glass of alcohol when you must drive home. By listening to these red flag feelings, practicing prudence helps us avoid walking the path of the gorged sheep, removing us from unhealthy behaviors or harmful situations.

A GOOD DANCE PARTNER

I've spent a lifetime dancing with prudence, learning to follow its lead. That gorged sheep made a deep impression on me because of my adolescent history with bulimia. I understand gorging yourself. I also know the dangers of not heeding warnings about our behaviors.

To live free of disordered eating, I've had to understand how uncomfortable emotions caused me to self-medicate with food. Knowing how to calm my emotions without food took a while; I was often reactive, turning to food when emotionally charged. Over several years, I've had to change my mindset, develop self-control, and learn healthier replacement behaviors. My dance with prudence continually moves back and forth in this and in all areas of my life.

Where do you need to follow prudence's lead? My particular struggle is with food and emotions. Yours might be with overspending, the inability to follow through on things, social media or porn addiction, or other potentially destructive behaviors. It's easy to dismiss prudence's importance because lack of caution is everywhere, even encouraged—in the environment, politics, media, and general social behavior. We don't see prudence modeled as frequently as in past generations.

But God provides an example of prudence in the Bible when he tells us to examine the ant. "Observe her ways and be wise, which, having no chief, overseer or ruler, she prepares her food in the summer and brings in her provisions . . . in the harvest" (Proverbs 6:6–8, AMP). Likewise, we also must be thoughtful about how our actions today determine future consequences, whether for benefit or detriment, without someone telling us what to do. This art of governing ourselves with reason and caution is lost in our impulsive culture. Let's relearn how to develop a prudent mindset.

A NEW MINDSET

Prudence starts with critical thinking about cause and effect. At school, we teach children to synthesize cause and effect in reading comprehension—*if Johnny does this, what will happen next?* But it's also an essential life skill too often crowded out by impulsivity, here-and-now living, and instant gratification. Like the gorged sheep, we see what we want, ignore caution to get it, and deal with results later. We need discernment to pause before acting and reacting.

A simple way to create the pause of prudence is through an exercise that children learn through *if-then* or *when-then* statements. *If* or *when* I do this, *then* this could be the outcome.

- *If* I eat the entire bag of Oreos, *then* my stomach will hurt.

- *When* I tell my preschooler no, *then* I must follow through and not give in.
- *If* I want to be considered for a promotion, *then* I must arrive on time.

You get the picture.

THE MIDDLE WAY

Some of you may think—*this will increase my anxiety! I'm already stuck in a debilitating loop of* if-then *thoughts.* It may seem counterintuitive, but prudence lessens stress because it calms an anxious brain. It partners the logical frontal lobe with the amygdala, our brain's emotional center. Like the ant, a prudent person sees a need or recognizes harm and takes the best next step, with calm caution, to meet that need or avoid danger. Prudence utilizes our natural processes to create a healthy, balanced lifestyle.

Let's go back to the middle lane analogy. Rather than weave back and forth between slow and fast lanes, creating more risks, you stay in the middle lane until your exit. You're not worrying about whom to pass or when to recenter. You can enjoy the ride and safely get to your destination on time.

I call it *the middle way*. It's the opposite of extreme thoughts and behavior. Instead, it's centered thinking and a balanced lifestyle—generations before called it wisdom and discernment. Then luxury, convenience, anxiety, and fatalism entered our world, tempting us into those outer lanes. We couldn't resist; now we've lost our reasonable minds.

A prudent mind is not overtaken by fear. Instead, it prompts us to pause, allowing the rational brain to talk to our emotions. It tells you that *if* you touch a hot stove, *then* you will get burned. It doesn't say to stay out of the kitchen and starve because of dangerous things. Prudence's pause invites you to listen to your head, body, and heart to consider what it's trying to tell you.

JUST BREATHE

Isaiah 18:4 gives a powerful visualization of this: "I will remain quiet and look on from my dwelling place." I love this image of prudent reflection as one considers what is coming up in the day.

I think of a farmer, before the weather app or Doppler radar, who steps outside his home, breathing in the day's air. He can tell from its smell and moisture that it might rain. He pauses and considers that rain will ruin the hay if he doesn't bail it and get it inside the barn. Cause and effect tell him bailing hay is his day's priority.

Prudence pauses to breathe, think, and consider. It can include formal mindfulness practices or breathing techniques. You might schedule five minutes of reflection in your day to organize your thoughts. I make time most mornings for journaling, Bible reading, and prayer, which help me collect my thoughts, process emotions, and think about the upcoming day or week.

When rushed, I use my forty-minute commute for silence, turning off the radio or podcasts. I think about my day, being thoughtful of unpredictable situations with students that may come up in which I will need wisdom. I am comforted by the promise in James 1:5 that God gives wisdom generously to those who ask. I often pray, "Lord, I don't know what this day will hold. But you do. Equip me with wisdom for what I need."

LIFE SKILLS 101

My dad was a middle-way man, as many were in the Silent Generation. They were children during the Great Depression, came of age during World War II, and lived through a post-war world of potential nuclear war. Shaped by these sobering events, they are cautious, steady, and prudent, saving things others throw away, just in case. You may have a middle-way person in your life, too.

I appreciated Dad's prudence when my sisters and I graduated from college. Before we moved out on our own, he taught us how to check the oil in a car, change a tire, and jump-start a dead car battery. I learned from him that it was prudent to travel with a map and keep your gas tank from getting below the red zone.

His lessons of prudence taught me caution and wisdom about new areas of life I didn't think about before. From him, I learned that prudence is not only in-the-moment thinking or planned reflection but essential knowledge for life maintenance.

MESSY LIVES

As a mental health professional, I've conducted home-based services for life skills in addition to therapy. One day, an individual told me I would know how they were doing by how their house looked. It was a statement about all our lives that I'll never forget. As I worked with them, cleaning and decluttering their physical and emotional spaces, I learned life lessons, too.

When you tidy up, you see your life and situation more clearly. But we live cluttered, overcrowded, and chaotic lives. Prudence is the master virtue because it brings order to all parts of your life. *If* you declutter a few minutes daily, *then* you won't be as overwhelmed. *If* you pause to think, *then* you won't send that mean text.

Small things in life matter. Making my bed daily, keeping clutter in a basket, and putting dishes away bring visual and internal order to my day. These tasks make me feel accomplished, especially when other tasks aren't completed or I have too many competing responsibilities. The chores take just a few minutes and aren't waiting for me when I come home from a hectic workday.

What easy steps can you take to declutter your physical and mental spaces? Your needs may be different than mine. But being prudent in small things helps with more significant issues, like addressing the internal chaos that can overwhelm us.

SCRIPTURE APPLICATION

For me, that internal chaos first manifested through the bulimia I struggled with as a teen and young adult. But God met me there. While reading my Bible in college, I came across 1 Corinthians 10:23, which says, "I have the right to do anything . . . but not everything is beneficial." It was a wise, cautious principle that applied directly to me. I had the freedom to act however I wanted, even when it was self-destructive. But it didn't benefit my physical, mental, or emotional health. The verse seems personified by that dead sheep on our barn floor.

Since college, this verse has not only helped me overcome disordered eating but has helped me change various mindsets and behaviors. Another biblical principle in overcoming bulimia is from 1 Corinthians 10:13, which says God will not allow you to be tempted beyond what you can handle. But when you are tempted, he will provide a way of escape.

This scripture helped me withstand temptations that lured me into those outer lanes of more destructive behavior. I knew I had safer options to handle hurt or dysregulated feelings when tempted by food or to purge. This promise has helped me in other areas of life where temptation drowns out the pause of discernment.

A PRUDENT LIFESTYLE

Ron, like my dad, learned prudence from his upbringing. There's no room for foolishness or carelessness on a farm. I learned that the first time I forgot to close the valve on the bulk milk tank, which stored a days' worth of milk, hard work, and income. After getting a gallon of raw milk out to take home for our family, I didn't check to see if I screwed the valve tight. Ron came home informing me that my carelessness sent money down the drain (literally).

I've learned to double-check important final steps ever since.

Life experiences teach discernment one way or another. Often, we make decisions out of impulsivity, fear, or worry. Prudence helps us consider long-term effects beyond immediate needs or anxieties.

Y2K was an impending possible crisis in 1999 when we built our house. People feared a computer glitch at the turn of the millennium would cause electricity grids, technology, and everything controlled by computers to crash. Survivalist precautions were rampant. Being pregnant, with three young kids, I feared having no heat, water, or electricity with a young family and a newborn in the Midwest winter.

I wanted to ensure we had working options in place for the possible crisis. Prudence, to me, looked like installing primitive systems in our new home, like a hand pump for water, in case modern technologies failed. However, Ron's idea of prudence was not changing permanent house plans for an event that might or might not happen.

With differing views on such long-term decisions, I had to assess if my plans were from caution or fear. What worried me most was not having water for a newborn's formula or food for our kids. I discerned our greatest needs and compromised by ensuring we had jugs of distilled water, more canned goods, and a few other staples on hand.

At the stroke of midnight on January 1, 2000, the world didn't end. Today I'm glad we didn't incur extra expenses for things we didn't really need. I've learned prudence is sharpened when we learn from differing perspectives, negotiate needs, and make decisions from wisdom, not fear.

LET GO OF FATALISM AND IDEALISM

Prudence balances worry and fear. It assesses needs, risks, and options and then plans accordingly. My professional friend helped me think through risks and ways to mitigate them. Ron discerned it was unwise to design a home based on fear. Pausing to consider cause and effect creates healthy, strategic planning. It avoids fatalism and idealism, often the two extremes we find ourselves caught between.

The biblical picture of idealism for most women is seen in Proverbs 31, the narrative of the woman who does everything. Looking at the passage through the lens of prudence, we see neither fear nor idealism but a woman caring for those around her with cautious, wise planning. Proverbs 31:25 says she laughs at the days to come—she can because she's been faithful to ensure her household and family are cared for. She isn't fearful, nor does she strive toward perfection, but she maintains a more carefree, secure middle lane lifestyle.

My friend Dorie found the Proverbs 31 balance when her husband was diagnosed with a terminal illness. At first, she cared for her husband while living in the tension of fear and idealism, trying to keep up with the matters left to her care in addition to work and family needs. *If-then* statements ran through her mind as she anticipated consequences if she slacked on the responsibilities. Her husband encouraged her to stop anticipating and just keep things simple to decrease her worry. She learned to live more in the present at his prompting, enjoying the restful pause of prudence.

You, too, can have a middle way lifestyle of caution and rest—it just requires practice. Spend more time pausing before you act. Slow down your thoughts. Be present, not restless, in the pause. Don't plan too far ahead, but take each situation as it arises, cautiously assessing what is best for each situation. Let's explore some examples.

CULTIVATE PRUDENCE

While on vacation alone, I went to a park to walk my dog and saw no other people around. I paused and wondered if walking in a deserted park was safe. With prudence, I drove my dog into the town and walked on neighborhood sidewalks instead.

An acquaintance, Robyn, learned from her oldest daughter's experience that being on social media too early had risks. So when her youngest daughter, Candice, begged to be on TikTok, she prudently talked through *if-then* scenarios with her. Candice then better understood and accepted her mom's age guidelines for social media.

Life teaches us if we are willing to learn. My friend Elizabeth has tried her hand at many endeavors over her adult life. She says, "Some things I've tried have worked, and some haven't. But I've found contentment in finding what does work." This process of learning is what prudence teaches us. It's not about having all the knowledge and taking calculated steps that go exactly as you hope. Nor is it a path of foolishness. It's a process of discerning and learning from daily life experiences.

Simply asking yourself, "What did I learn?" gathers a lifetime of lessons that inform personal and professional choices. Eva Goble from *Memories of Hoosier Homemakers* says learning makes life significant: "If you're not learning, you're already out of business."[5] She and Elizabeth teach us that a lifestyle of prudence builds a pathway of growth, safety, and freedom.

Let's see how we can cultivate an enjoyable and prudent middle way lifestyle.

SIMPLE SECRETS: NEXT STEPS

Now it's your turn. Here are simple suggestions to practice prudence and uncomplicate your life.

- Write a to-do list of things that must be done today, this week, and in upcoming weeks.
- Make a budget in an area of spending in which you struggle. Then live accordingly.
- List two things you would like to declutter from your life so you have more time or energy. Perhaps you can delete a social media app, reduce unwanted responsibilities, or teach your children to pick up.
- Journal *if-then*, or *when-then* statements concerning upcoming decisions, present problems, or fears. Be realistic about potential outcomes.
- Take a class on finances, nutrition, self-defense, household management, or other areas in which you would like to be more prudent.
- Post a quote or Bible verse somewhere that reminds you to pause or avoid impulsivity.
- Schedule preventative appointments such as mammograms, yearly physicals, or counseling sessions.
- See a doctor or counselor if you struggle with an ongoing lack of focus or impulsivity.

- Set aside five to ten minutes daily to pause and reflect on your day or week. Be curious about what you have learned.
- Trace your hand and breathe in on the upstrokes and out on the downstrokes to create a pause. This decreases racing thoughts and trains your mind, heart, and body to pause.

Prayer pause: *Invite Jesus to reveal what he desires for you from this chapter.*

REFLECTION

1. Do you struggle with fatalism or idealism? What next step can you take to be more centered in middle-way mindsets?
2. Who in your life exemplifies prudence? How would you like to emulate them?
3. What did you learn that is most helpful, or what reflects your needs and hopes in this chapter? How will you apply that to your life?
4. What is one lesson of prudence from your life that you can retell to another person?

Chapter 4

Simple Common Sense

Without vision, you don't see, and without practicality, the bills don't get paid.

—Paul Engle[1]

I looked out the window of my toddler's bedroom, which I was painting. Outside, Ron and his dad were putting in a split rail fence that framed the backyard around our newly built home. Feeling frustrated and misunderstood, my tears fell freely.

The fence's location was a significant disagreement Ron and I had when we built our home in the former cow pasture. With such wide-open space, I envisioned a big shaded lawn, like that at Grandpa's house, which sloped down to a creek on the north side where our kids could play, like out of a story-book. Ron, however, had different ideas.

My dream, to him, was impractical. It meant less pasture and fresh water for the heifers. A large backyard meant more grass to mow. We could still use the idyllic space for play and

picnics; we'd just have to dodge the cow patties. Many frustrating conversations in our marriage went this way. I'd have
visionary ideas, and Ron kept fencing them in.

For years, I had maintained a careful budget for our family
on one income, snatching 50-percent-off deals, shopping at
thrift stores, and pinching pennies where I could. I had hoped
for a little bit of frill when we got to build a brand-new home.
We already scored an A-plus in practicality and cost efficiency
by having high schoolers build it.

But as the plans came together, we often disagreed. Like
many farmers, Ron was raised to be pragmatic. Each cost or
decision affects your livelihood on a farm. If you can save
money, you do, along with trying to get the most value for
something you may purchase. You save on other expenses by
doing a lot of work with your own two hands. If you can
grow, build, or do it yourself, that's what you do. Practical
skills are the bedrock of our community.

BACK TO BASICS

When supply chains were disrupted during the pandemic,
people flocked to our area for back-to-basics resources. Our
hardware stores sell things like Granite Ware canners and
meat grinders that help people make more essentials at home.

But most people today don't need meat-grinding skills—we
need the practical processes they represent. We need skills to
earn money for the meat, buy it at a reasonable price, cook it,
and clean the dishes afterward. Basic life skills our grandparents
and parents would have taken for granted have been displaced
by technology, convenience, and immediate gratification.

We even view these simpler skills and processes as overwhelming impediments to our busy lives. I was surprised when
my kids first introduced me to the term *adulting*. When did

being an adult become a verb? It used to be an expectation of life. Let's uncomplicate your life by teaching you some old-fashioned practicality.

PRACTICALITY: THE FOURTH SECRET

Having life skills and knowing how to use them is the most fundamental definition of the fourth secret: practicality. These skills include household, employment, health, financial, and consumer aptitudes. Some may call these mindsets and behaviors *common sense* or *pragmatism*. They are not theoretical, speculative, or abstract. Our forebearers didn't stand around and pose theories about how to feed their families or fix a leaking roof. They considered the most cost-effective way to do it, then did the next thing.

While practical skills differ depending on your environment, basic life skills are the same. We humans have similar needs and processes, no matter where we live. On a trip to India, the group I traveled with visited a home when it was time to milk the water buffalo. The homeowner asked if anyone wanted to try milking. I volunteered, squatting in my khakis and dress shirt, among the dung and flies, and started milking like I did at home. The moment was a sacred lesson that taught me the universality of basic human tasks, regardless of our differences. Practical skills are human skills, regardless of education, position, or location.

BEAUTIFUL YET FUNCTIONAL

Though Ron and I have sparred over my visionary ideas and his pragmatism, I've learned a practical lifestyle can be creative and beautiful. The first summer I was married, Ron's mom bought me a flat of young flower seedlings for my birthday. She taught me how to plant them by digging holes, pouring water, putting the flower in, and covering it with dirt. Our honeymoon home was transformed as the flowers grew with vibrant red, pink, and yellow colors. I quickly grew a love for flowers and gardening, a luxury of little cost but extravagant beauty.

When we moved to our new home, I saw how the unwanted fence could be the perfect backdrop for a perennial flower garden, but Ron cautioned me of its impracticality. The former pasture's soil was filled with tree roots and native Indiana prairie grass. Planting flowers and having them survive was iffy.

Determined, I used the garden tiller to tear up the roots and sod. I dumped five-gallon buckets of fresh cow manure on top of the ground. Barefoot and pregnant (I'm not kidding), I walked back and forth behind the garden tiller mixing the compost into the soil, transforming it into a beautiful garden. Over twenty years later, those perennial flowers still bloom all summer long. Pragmatism creates beautiful yet functional spaces.

BENEFITS OF COST ANALYSIS

Practicality also means appreciating the value of things. One of our Gen Z kids is a minimalist; when he purchases something, he knows why and is willing to spend money on it and take care of it. This feels like a rarity in a culture increasingly shaped by consumption, where items are made cheaply, assuming that we'll move on to the next thing quickly. But cost analysis was ingrained in past generations. My father spent a lot of money on well-made bedroom furniture when he and my mom married. He grew up without ever having a bed of his own. My mom still uses that stylish 1950s furniture.

In contrast, many Americans spend impulsively, which often results in unwanted purchases or debt. When our kids were young, we tried to teach them cost analysis so they would know the difference between needs and wants, practical and luxury items, and the value of each. The kids partially paid for large purchases, such as gaming systems and electronics, with money saved from birthdays or chores. We continued this principle of jointly sharing the costs of other big-ticket items, like a college education.

Cost analysis looks different for each family. However it's done, instilling earned value and financial prudence are important for children and grandchildren. Kids need to know the cost involved in a product or process and the work required to obtain what they want.

GETTING THE JOB DONE

One year when I was teaching US history, my class wanted to bury a time capsule. I made the dream a practical reality by purchasing the time capsule and having the students gather the items they felt were important to inform a future generation. Next we had to complete the project by burying the time capsule.

I involved each class in the process, bringing a wheelbarrow, shovel, tarp, and post-hole digger from home. My students were surprised when I didn't back away from the hard work of shoveling and digging in the dirt. They were accustomed to seeing me in skirts and heels, not as a gardener or farmer's wife who gets her hands dirty with practical, menial work.

Getting your hands dirty is a euphemism for getting things done, in contrast to speculating or discussing ideas from a distance. This is how practical skills differ from academic ideas—they involve getting in there and using your hands. Burying a time capsule was a great idea; finishing the job meant being willing to do the dirty work.

Practical skills are common among our community's Amish. Unlike mainstream culture, the Amish value practical skills and applied arts, traditionally attending school only through the eighth grade before they begin full-time work on or off the farm. Yet many are innovative and wise entrepreneurs. Their work ethic, resourcefulness, and folk knowledge can't be taught in the classroom.

Similar skills, though, are making a valued comeback. According to the *Harvard Business Review*, more specific skills-based hiring should open over one million jobs for non-college degree holders in the next few years.[2] Job seekers are questioning traditional higher education with a tight labor market, the cost of college, increased living expenses, and a declining economic outlook. Employers are discovering that the best workers may have valuable skills other than a formal degree.

YOU'VE GOT WHAT IT TAKES

These functional skills are being sought out in our homes, too. A friend texted me a social media meme saying we need more skills that our grandmothers knew, not advice from twenty-something influencers.[3] It resonated with me. When I speak to groups of moms, one of the most requested topics is managing time, household responsibilities, marriage, and raising kids—areas of expertise for our grandmothers.

A few years ago, I held a sold-out conference for moms overwhelmed and eager to learn practical skills to manage their busy lives. The content evolved into a book entitled *Balance, Busyness, and Not Doing It All.* While raising four kids, our household was full and chaotic at times, with me as a stay-at-home and working mom plus Ron teaching and dairy farming.

I'm grateful for the practical skills other moms and I learned in the pre-internet days, such as learning to improvise a recipe or trusting our intuition with childhood illness rather than running to Google for such things. We didn't have instant answers when we had questions, but we had to figure things out before calling someone for advice. These and other experiences provided a foundation for managing family life.

In contrast, you may question your instinctive abilities, though they are just as sharp as your grandmother's. Social media fuels comparison to Superwomen influencers and the ideal Instagram life rather than equipping you to trust yourself with practical knowledge and processes women have used for generations. You have what it takes to make wise, practical decisions! One way to step into this is to control the messages you surround yourself with.

Be selective about whose online voices influence you, determining what value their content or presence brings to your life. Spend more time in Scripture rather than scrolling. Ask an older woman in your social network to teach you a skill or share her life lessons. By being selective of the voices in your life, you'll become the voice of reason to someone else.

YOU HAVE CHOICES

Another struggle in practical decision-making is the fear of making mistakes. When I spoke with Bridget, a graduating senior overwhelmed by college decisions, she shared that both she and her mom were worried about making the wrong choice. I suggested she consider alternate options rather than choosing a college she wasn't sure of simply because she felt she had to. Bridget could work a year or more until she was sure about her next steps. "We didn't think it could be that simple," Bridget's mom said. They were relieved to consider practical alternatives.

We often complicate our lives by overthinking situations and making them more difficult than they need to be, such as thinking there is only one choice for a life path, rather than many. When we face difficult decisions or feel we don't have good options, considering all practical choices decreases anxiety. Without viable options, we feel trapped and out of control. Knowing how to apply practical next steps to make progress toward any life, career, relationship, or health goal provides the control and hope we long for.

When my coworker Annie and I introduce ourselves to students at the beginning of a school year, we tell them that we, as school counselors, don't magically make their problems disappear. However, we help them practically problem-solve what they can control. Sometimes the most basic solutions include regulating their emotions, knowing when to ask for help, and developing healthy coping skills at school.

Such practical tools benefit both kids and adults. Unfortunately, it's often easier to avoid our problems. Video games, social media, and virtual reality provide immediate escape pathways into a fantasy world that takes us away from discomfort. The mental health crisis among youth and young adults is impacted by the rising amount of screen time devoted to these distractions, which leads to an inability to cope with problems that don't disappear.

YOUR NATURAL SUPERCOMPUTER

The good news is that we all can develop practical, healthier skills. God gave us everything we need for a safe, vibrant life with the human processes he created—our intellect, reason, and discernment. Our brain is the most amazing organ designed by our Creator—it's our natural supercomputer. When we use it to practice prudence, equanimity, and pragmatism, we feel more hopeful, confident, and in control. It provides us with common sense that assists our next steps when we feel helpless or overwhelmed. Let me share an example.

I have always traveled with maps when driving alone, but I've grown comfortable with only my Google Maps phone app lately. After speaking at an event in a Chicago suburb, I went shopping and didn't realize the charge in my phone was low. My phone battery was dead when I got in my car to drive home.

I panicked and felt helpless. I didn't know how to get from the shopping mall to the interstate without GPS or a physical map, or a phone to call for help. It would take a while to charge my phone with my car running in the parking lot to pull up a map. (I had a practical older car with a slow car charge.)

I tried to remember what resources I used before GPS. Most mall stores would not have maps, and employees may be unable to provide directions. What nearby businesses might have an employee who could explain how to get to the interstate or a computer to print directions? I found a realtor's office and explained my situation to the receptionist. Not only did she print MapQuest directions, but she also wrote down landmarks the old-fashioned way.

This experience reminded me how important practical problem solving is, especially without technology. Prior generations had to think on their feet without the crutch of technology. They didn't have cell phones in hand to call for help or Google to research what to do next. What they did have is God's supercomputer—their brain—that was filled with life experiences to inform a situation.

You have this resource, too. Life experiences, strengths, and skills in one area of your life are transferable resources for others. For example, being an athlete in high school gives you a skill set for teamwork, determination, and discipline on the job. Taking care of an ill child or parent, or marketing a small online business are transferable skills that can help in other personal and professional areas. Let's learn how to access our supercomputer's resources to build a practical mindset.

A NEW MINDSET

A practical mindset weighs the cost-effectiveness of nonrenewable resources: money, time, and energy. You can't get these precious commodities back once you use them. How you spend them either simplifies or complicates your life.

As with prudence, practical thinking uses *if-then* and *when-then* processes, weighing realistic outcomes for choices before you. *When* I run errands in one trip, *then* I have more time to hang out with friends. *If* I pay cash, *then* I won't have debt.

An easy way to grow a practical mindset is to ask yourself whether the outcome you're about to pursue with your resources is a need or a want. What will result if you spend your time, money, or energy? Is it worth the investment? Are there other options?

Another factor is weighing short-term and long-term goals. Sometimes it's more practical to hold off on a purchase or decision because it benefits a long-term plan. Or a practical short-term decision may meet an immediate need that is helpful for the future. The answers to these questions are unique to you and your situation and require knowing what exactly you want out of your life, both now and in the future. Sometimes others may not understand your decision, and you need to be okay with that.

YOU'RE DOING WHAT?

It may have looked impractical to onlookers for me to leave a full-time teaching career to attend graduate school when I had four kids at home. Our oldest was approaching college, also. But our long-term goal was that I could have more job opportunities for flexible employment while our kids were home.

For the three years while I was in graduate school, life was crazy. I drove two hours daily to complete compatible programs at two universities that would eventually allow me to work as a licensed therapist or school counselor. The investment in those hectic years paid off. They have made many job opportunities possible, which have changed as our family needs have also changed.

More schools now provide practical education options that give students alternate life paths and choices. High school career academies provide certification in trades like dental hygiene and mechanics. Dual credit enrollment programs are popular, allowing high school students to begin earning college credit early. Some universities offer accelerated pathways for students to graduate in three years instead of four. Like any investment, education should be approached practically in addition to following dreams or passions.

But practical choices don't have to be as dramatic as changing careers or quitting a job. They are daily choices that simplify life. Whether we recognize it or not, our schedules align with our priorities. You can make more time for what is most important to you by making simple changes. Ordering grocery pick-up, decluttering, planning meals, or having kids help with household responsibilities—the little things make life smoother.

SCRIPTURE APPLICATION

The Bible has much to say about practicality. Luke 15:11–32 tells the story of the prodigal son who foolishly misuses resources. Psalms, Proverbs, and Ecclesiastes often contrast wisdom and foolishness. The following verses provide similar glimpses of practical or foolish lifestyles:

> The wise can see where they are going, but fools walk in the dark (Ecclesiastes 2:14, NLT).

> Wise people think before they act; fools don't—and even brag about their foolishness (Proverbs 13:16, NLT).

> The way of fools seems right to them, but the wise listen to advice (Proverbs 12:15).

Another biblical principle is to present your practical needs to God in prayer. Then practice praise. Remember Philippians 4:6–7? Its simple steps walk you through this process: "Do not be anxious about anything, but in every situation, by prayer and petition, with thanksgiving, present your requests to God. And the peace of God, which transcends all understanding, will guard your hearts and your minds in Christ Jesus."

George Müller is known for living by such practical prayer for his needs. He was a nineteenth-century evangelist in England who founded an orphanage. He routinely presented daily needs to God on behalf of the orphans, only to have the needs practically met.[4] I am challenged by stories like this to go to God daily with my ordinary needs.

God supplies every detailed need of our lives when we come to him. This doesn't mean he answers every prayer in the way we desire. However, he supplies us with a supernatural peace, hope, and provision in unexpected ways. In *Streams in the Desert*, Lettie Cowman says it is well to close every prayer praising God for the answer he has already given because he never forsakes his loving kindness and truth.[5] Praise and petition build up our faith.

A PRACTICAL LIFESTYLE

A practical lifestyle is easier with gratitude and contentment. Practicality can be winsome, creative, and fun when you have a full-to-overflowing attitude. A practical lifestyle makes you curious; follow that curiosity to learn how to plant something, use a power drill, or make your home more functional. When I went to graduate school, I needed a quiet place to study. We moved the children's bedrooms around and created space for a home office I otherwise would not have considered possible.

Practical creativity abounds in all life stages. Annika is a single, busy career woman who uses weekly grocery pick-ups to leverage her valuable time outside work. Cali, a stay-at-home mom, shops at thrift stores for gently used items. Kalyn hires someone within her budget to clean her home so she can be available for her children's sporting events on the weekends.

We all have different needs. What may be perceived as a luxury to one person—such as housecleaning services or other time-saving conveniences—could be very practical for another with different priorities around time or energy. Making practical choices requires knowing yourself, your needs, and what is most valuable to you.

And simple daily practices go a long way toward uncomplicating your life. Picking up while coffee is brewing or having organized totes are helpful for all. When our kids were young, I'd pick up the day's toys at naptime and bedtime. It usually took about five minutes, but I felt less overwhelmed by not seeing the work that needed to be done. Identifying these simple, regular tasks can help alleviate your daily stress and excess burdens.

LET GO OF EXCESS

Excess—whether too much information, too much stuff, or too many choices—may be the biggest obstacle to pragmatism.

Letting go of all the extra things in our minds, hearts, and dashboard of options allows us to see beautiful, simplified, and less complicated choices.

For example, shopping at big box stores is very distracting for me. One day after returning from an overseas mission trip, I was in the cereal aisle at Walmart. I was instantly overwhelmed by the excess choices in cereal compared to the needs I'd just witnessed in a different culture. I just needed some Cheerios in the yellow box. There were more types of Cheerios than I thought imaginable. The sheer volume of options made a simple task stressful.

You can begin to let go of this excess by intentionally simplifying your choices, especially with all the available options and ever more sophisticated targeted ads. Scrolling your phone feeds excess information into your brain and complicates your thoughts and feelings about your options. Comparing your messy house to the carefully curated Instagram posts of others makes you feel like you're doing something wrong. You're not. When you remove these unrealistic expectations, you can more easily lean into what's best for you.

There are other excesses to let go of—excess stuff and excess information. You can declutter your house, a few minutes at a time, to make a noticeable difference. You can also limit the websites you visit or podcasts you listen to so your mind is also free from extra "stuff."

Lastly, let go of impulse buying, which contributes to excess things you don't need, from online subscriptions to big-ticket items. Waiting at least a day before purchasing something you weren't planning on saves your sensibility, pocketbook, and shelf space. Advertising is meant to tap into our pleasure centers and convince us that we can't live without this one thing. If you give time for that feeling to fade, it will become clearer whether this is something you actually need or that will help you get where you'd like to go.

CULTIVATING PRACTICALITY

I retreated to a state park a few years ago and spent a beautiful afternoon by a lake. It was my practical rhythm of self-stewardship before an upcoming busy season. Sitting by the water was calming and restorative. What would it be like to regularly retreat to a quiet waterfront, I wondered? Buying a lake cottage wasn't a realistic option for us. But we did have a creek just beyond our fence. So twenty years after my original request that had lost out to Ron's practicality, I made my case.

"Ron, we are midlife. We don't know how many years we are guaranteed good health. I spent a peaceful day by the water, and it would not be complicated to have such an experience like that at home. We can't afford a lake property, but we have a beautiful creek just over the fence. Moving the fence to the other side of it wouldn't cost much. We could put our yard swing right by it where we could sit and enjoy it."

Ron took his hat off and scratched his head (which, for some farmers, means something is doable but not practical) A few days later, while I was speaking out of town, he sent me a photo of the hole where a fence post had just been. Within a few days, he moved the fence by digging new post holes on the other side of the creek and repositioning it. We now have a beautiful, restful spot with a yard swing and hammock overlooking our creek, just like a storybook. And it's cow-patty-free.

Pragmatism beautifies, simplifies, and keeps you grounded. Our kids have all driven cheaper, older used cars that they could afford when in high school and college. A few years ago, a friend drove by our house when all the kids were home for the summer. She texted me, "The kids must be home. Your driveway looks like a used car lot."

I laughed, but it was true. Practical living uncomplicates your life because, among other things, it builds character.

SIMPLE SECRETS: NEXT STEPS

Now it's your turn. Here are simple suggestions to practice practicality and uncomplicate your life:

- Make a list of three practical skills you would like to develop. It may be growing tomatoes, changing a tire, or ordering your first grocery pickup. Plan it. Then do it.
- Identify one time-sucking activity in your schedule that you can delegate.
- Set a timer for seven minutes twice a day and declutter in one area. Then rotate different places each day.
- Wait a day the next time you want to make an impulse purchase.
- Have a practical party—invite a few friends and share your best household or life hacks!
- Multitask, such as running errands on one day rather than several.
- Answer emails at the end of the day, rather than the beginning.
- Teach your kids one practical skill each week or month. Some suggestions include reading a map, making a bed, writing a résumé, estimating a tip, or entertaining themselves without technology.
- Ask your mom, grandma, or an older woman for their most practical tips.
- Incorporate one way to lessen your carbon footprint.

Prayer pause: *Invite Jesus to reveal what he desires for you from this chapter.*

REFLECTION

1. In what area of your life would you like to grow practical skills? What's your best next step to do so?
2. Who is one person in your life who models pragmatism? What do you learn from them or would you like to emulate?
3. What did you learn from this chapter that is most helpful, or what reflects your needs and hopes? How will you apply that to your life?
4. What is one lesson of pragmatism from your life that you can retell to another person?

Chapter 5

Unsung Heroes

God has not called us to be successful, but to be faithful.
—Mother Teresa[1]

I was nineteen and home for summer break from college when Lois, Ron's mom, asked if I would come with her to clean the apartment of an older woman from our community. We piled cleaning supplies, brooms, and mops into her car and drove to the local senior citizen center.

Ellen was around ninety years old. Her small one-room efficiency apartment had water damage from a recent storm. She felt overwhelmed by the work she could no longer do by herself. The cement walls needed to be wiped down, along with other things. Her only child lived several states away.

Ellen was a widow of the older Mennonite tradition. She wore dresses and a prayer covering on her head. As I washed walls and cleaned around her, I asked her to tell me about her family. She unexpectedly told me her husband had left her for another woman several years before. "I never divorced him. I made a vow to God and James." We chatted some more about the quilt she was making and other daily happenings. But the dynamics of her story—her steadfast fidelity despite a broken marriage that took place long ago before no-fault divorce—spoke loudly to me as a young adult who rarely witnessed such authentic commitment.

On the ride home, Lois shared that Ellen donated land from the farm she and James had owned to a local church after he died. Ellen's witness of how her faith guided her life kept drawing me back to visit her until she passed away. Her humble demeanor and fidelity to God still influence me today.

Ellen is one of many women and men whose lives compel me to live like them. They are heroes because they are true to their word, show up when things are hard, and do the most sacred tasks when no one is looking. Their lives embody the beauty of fidelity.

HOPE IN HARD TIMES

In looking at the lives of these unsung heroes, we witness hope—not the fluffy, feel-good kind often witnessed on social media. Hope is a by-product of fidelity, loyalty, and faithfulness, and it stands out among the brokenness in our culture—broken promises, broken hearts, broken systems, and broken relationships. I see how these individual and systemic problems directly affect my students. It's debilitating some days, wondering if there's anyone who does what's right for the sake of integrity. You see it, too, in your workplace, in politics, on the news, and in personal relationships.

I was encouraged during the 2020–2021 school year by the fidelity of school leaders who ensured the safety of staff and students while we maintained in-person learning. That year gave me hope that people still do the right thing even in difficult and trying circumstances. I was inspired by the old-fashioned stick-with-it-ness that was the order of the day. I saw fidelity, *that something,* that holds the fabric of families and communities together.

FIDELITY: THE FIFTH SECRET

You may think of fidelity—the fifth secret—as important only in a marriage. It's much more. Fidelity is continued loyalty to someone or something, evidenced by reliability, trustworthiness, and ongoing support. Ellen was loyal to her vows and God, even when her husband was not. School leaders and colleagues I worked with were reliable and trustworthy in doing what was best for kids and one another during the pandemic.

Treat people right and do the right thing is another way to explain fidelity. That phrase was the signature line of a former principal I worked for. It's what my dad lived in a generation where it was scandalous if you did anything different.

Fidelity includes keeping promises. A teacher once described fidelity as, "A *said* is a *said.*" There is no need to say, "I promise," because your actions follow your words, like a handshake. In past generations, a handshake was a promise, and a person's word was their honor.

Both my parents and in-laws were of the handshake era. They were from the Silent Generation, those born between 1928 and 1945. As a whole, their generation was known for being hard workers and pragmatics. They were loyal to their employers, family, and the values they were raised with. They valued doing what was right when no one was looking.

I once asked Dad, an insurance agent, what caused him to move our family from one city to another. He said his employer asked him to cheat a client by changing numbers. "I wouldn't do that," he said. He came home that night and told my mom he quit his job. A few weeks later, they relocated.

ACTIONS SPEAK

I never knew that story until the later years of Dad's life. Most acts of fidelity are practiced in life's quiet, intimate moments. We usually don't witness them. But we notice *that something* when we see it, especially in today's nefarious and disloyal culture.

Ron's dad, Bob, was on dialysis for the last year of his life. He was hospitalized when his body could not withstand another treatment. Knowing death was imminent, as siblings we took turns being with him in the hospital. We often sang hymns or prayed with him.

A nurse who took care of him mentioned to me how rare it was for a patient to have family members attending in such a way. Her comment highlighted how relationships have become me-centered rather than other-centered. Acts of fidelity speak loudly in empty rooms and lonely hearts. Caring for Bob was an ordinary act, but like Ellen did with me, it made an impression on someone else.

OUT WITH THE OLD, IN WITH THE NEW

The Silent Generation's cultural fidelity has been replaced by self-centeredness, instant gratification, and untethered relationships. Ironically, Gen Z, today's young adults, have been compared to the Silent Generation. They have lived through two economic crises and a twenty-year war against terrorism, came of age during the pandemic, and have not known a world without mass shootings.

We can learn from them. Gen Z young people are more practical and risk-averse than their older siblings, the Millennials. They are engaging more in their culture to make a difference. They may surprise us as they enter the workforce, politics, and education, and as they raise families. Their old but new ways may be the countercultural force that drives the pendulum of stability back to the center.

PERFECT PITCH

Visitors to our Amish community often marvel at the Amish fidelity to their lifestyle. The Amish still struggle with the same human feelings that we English do, but their fidelity to their community guides and empowers them. With each cultural challenge, they must ask critical questions, including, "What will this do to our community?" They know that each degree away from their original design changes things. Therefore decisions about what is best for the whole group are weighed in tension with individualism and autonomy.

I'm reminded of this when singing a cappella hymns. Our Mennonite congregation used a pitch pipe for years to start songs. Your ear attunes to the pitch, and you learn to harmonize with those around you. It creates beautiful four-part harmony. Slowly, piano accompaniment replaced a cappella singing. Then unison praise songs became more common. Over time, the ability to harmonize and match perfect pitch may be lost if the practice is abandoned completely.

It's a mirror of what happens over time in society. Commitments to values, ethics, and relationships similarly change when we alter beliefs or behaviors one degree, then another, and another. It's not that you can't be flexible or should cling to legalism or religious traditions. Instead, fidelity draws you back to that perfect pitch, tuning your ear and heart to the center of what you know to be true and good.

THOSE WHO SHOW UP

The pandemic changed our social DNA by isolating and separating us, and technology makes it easy to avoid integrated relationships. It takes effort to reorient ourselves with that perfect pitch of other-centered fidelity. What does the virtue even look like?

People who practice fidelity do what is best for others. They are present when things are hard. They are not fair-weather friends or transactional in their relationships.

My friend Jillian is one whose life leaves such an imprint, though she would never say so. Her fidelity to others made an impression on me soon after we met. Her mother abandoned her and her siblings when she was young, but still Jillian tended to her mother when she was sick and dying. I've witnessed Jillian similarly caring for others in adverse circumstances. She shows up for the people and the causes most important to her.

Fidelity doesn't just flit onto the scene. It's evidenced over time. I remind those who have been betrayed by someone that trust is not immediately built and should not be immediately returned. Apologizing doesn't change a person. Trust can be earned back only when they consistently live differently.

The best example of fidelity is God's unwavering faithfulness and goodness to us despite humanity's unfaithfulness to him. 1 John 1:9 says when we confess our sins, God is faithful and just to forgive us of our sins and will cleanse us from all unrighteousness. Hebrews 13:5 says God will not leave us or forsake us—he consistently shows up whether we acknowledge his presence or not. Most trustworthy is Jesus' salvation covenant which cannot be broken. God's promises are sure—his *said* is a *said*.

HUMANKIND'S BEST FRIEND

One example of fidelity captured worldwide attention in 2021. Boncuk the dog made headlines when he waited six days outside the entrance of a Turkish hospital while his owner was hospitalized. His family retrieved him daily, but each day he escaped and returned to the hospital until his caretaker was released.[2]

We humans can learn a lot about loyalty from animals. They have a sense for those who show up daily to care for them and are loyal to them in return. Our Airbnb guests are sometimes disappointed when our goats don't come to the fence for the visitors to pet them. This isn't a surprise—guests are strangers, and goats are somewhat aloof. But the girls will come in a heartbeat if Ron is at the gate.

The faithful relationship between caretakers and animals is the order of life on a farm. Ignoring an animal's care has detrimental consequences. An animal that doesn't come up to its feeder to eat indicates illness, which could result in death if not treated. A farmer's attentive care goes beyond water and food; it is a tender responsibility that calls you to duty at all hours of the day and night.

CIVIC DUTY

Fidelity is witnessed in city life, too. I observed different types of fidelity growing up in town. One example is civic fidelity my parents modeled by serving on various boards, county councils, and town government. My mom was Shipshewana town board president in the 1980s and 1990s, and again, decades later, when someone was needed to finish the term of a board president who had died. At age eighty-four, my mom stepped up to fill that need and was the town council president of one of the largest Midwest tourist towns. In 2021, the board created a civic lifetime achievement award in her name. They honored and commissioned her as the first recipient a few months after my dad died.

Community fidelity comes in all shapes and sizes. For you, it may mean serving on your local school board or volunteering for the PTO. It may look like initiating environmentally conscious practices in your business or donating time, work, or finances for a community need.

Several years ago, a teaching colleague of mine died of brain cancer. She was a single mom of two college-aged children. To support her family, the school had a fundraising carnival and wanted to give her kids a gift representing our love for her. We decided to give her kids a keepsake quilt that students and staff could sign at the carnival.

I knew our community would come through—two quilt store owners donated handmade quilts. On the carnival night, we displayed the quilts and dozens of people wrote notes describing how Lori impacted their lives.

Not all acts of fidelity are as elaborate, but they all are nonetheless important. In your community, fidelity's heroes may be the woman leading vacation Bible school year after year, the school crossing guard protecting children in all kinds of weather, or the retired woman who babysits for her neighbor's children. Fidelity is also lived out in quiet spaces: the meal you make for a friend, the hours in the church nursery, or the encouraging note you write to your single friend. You and other heroes don't make the news, but by seeing a need and following through, you make our communities work.

EQUITY OVER EQUALITY

I had all eleventh- and twelfth-grade students when I taught US history and government. I attempted to keep consistent standards for each teen, without showing favoritism, no matter their social, economic, or academic status. I tried to remove barriers so all students could succeed if they tried. For example, a student could handwrite a report if they could not access a computer at home.

Not giving special treatment outside of the consistent standards wasn't always popular. At the end of one school year, I was surprised to receive a note from a class leader. She thanked me for being fair in the classroom, acknowledging that it wasn't always easy. It taught me that people really do watch our ordinary behavior.

I didn't know at the time that what she witnessed was equity, which is another quality of fidelity. Equity means each person receives what they need to succeed. Equity recognizes that not everyone starts at the same place. Many of us have more resources than others, so the playing field for success is not equal due to circumstances, resources, capacity, or bias. What may be best or fair for one person is not necessarily best or fair for another.

In India, I met a washerwoman whose job was to do laundry by hand. I asked my host why the woman did not use a washing machine or a wringer washer, which would have been easier. My host shared Mahatma Gandhi's belief that everyone should have equity in society by having a job at their capacity. The washerwoman's manual skills were valued, and she could earn a living wage at her economic ability rather than a machine replacing her job. She was given a viable role in her community that modern processes and efficiency would have otherwise eliminated.

I wish we could replicate this in every community—doing the right thing for the right reasons because it's best for individuals *and* the whole group. Most often, we look out for ourselves, our financial interests, ease and efficiency, or the influential majority. Or we overlook those whose voices or needs are not immediately before us.

Jesus provides a better model. He *saw* people, meeting them where they were. He faithfully met individual needs while fostering healthy, compassionate norms for the broader community. Whether we recognize its significance, you and I do this in small ways. In families, it is adapting expectations based on a child's maturity or developmental needs. Or it is giving an older adult the best quality of life within their capacity. We follow Jesus' example each time we pause to make space for someone where they can thrive in their sphere of community.

BROKEN PROMISES

Stephen Covey says integrity conforms reality to your words.[3] To me, that is what Ellen's marriage commitment exemplified. This is not a blanket statement to justify or promote staying in toxic or abusive marriages. That is not fidelity. Fidelity is choosing to stay in a less-than-perfect relationship because it's the right thing to do; it honors God and those involved. Legalism, abuse, shame, or manipulation never honor God or others.

Some marriages end too soon. Reality TV shows have glamorized weddings without giving realistic expectations that relationships are also hard work and require commitment. Some colleges perpetuate a "get a ring by spring" culture that may idealize marriage without preparing young adults with the fidelity needed for a lifetime relationship.

On the opposite extreme, marriage in the larger culture has been displaced by relationships without fidelity. Hookups and polyamorous, transactional, and open relationships are socially acceptable, while monogamous marriages now comprise less than half of current couples. More people cohabitate, are sexually active but single, or have children with more than one partner. As family structures change, so do the relational commitments accompanying them.[4]

But even though social mores have changed, our human need for trustworthy, loyal relationships hasn't. In the face of these fragmenting relationships, we see that loneliness is now increasing, while face-to-face connection is decreasing. Fair-weather friends are more common than faithful ones. We are more devoted to posting about our daily adventures than calling, texting, or visiting someone we care about. Yet, deep down, this is what we hunger for.

A NEW MINDSET

I bought a pair of rocking chairs for our front porch a few years ago. They symbolized fidelity and long-term commitment in our marriage during a season of frustration and conflict. I imagined Ron and me in the sunset years of life, sitting in front porch rockers, grateful we stuck with our marriage and commitment to one another when it would have been easy to give up. Rocking chair goals became my marriage goals.

But I had to do the hard work of commitment. It's easy to internalize messages that life is about being happy at all costs. Such mindsets distract us from persevering through relationship struggles. We focus on what's negative rather than the assets in the relationship. When things are hard, giving up is always easier.

When negative thoughts about my marriage fueled a half-empty cup perspective, I memorized and dwelt on Philippians 4:8. It says, "Whatever is true, whatever is noble, whatever is right, whatever is pure, whatever is lovely, whatever is admirable—if anything is excellent or praiseworthy—think about such things." I often reviewed each quality, applying it to the situations, feelings, and thoughts that troubled me.

Reflecting on God's word transformed my thoughts and feelings into a positive truth. I began to focus on the best attributes of our marriage, not the worst. I imagined Ron and me sitting in the rocking chairs in later years, saying, "That was a rough time. I'm glad we persevered and made it through."

A LIFESTYLE OF FIDELITY

Fidelity is *that something* you can't quite put your finger on, but you know it when you see it. It makes you want it, too. It's why you are faithful to an obligation, responsibility, or person. But for those who need to see it modeled, a powerful story helps.

One of my favorite children's stories is *The Three Questions* by Jon J. Muth.[5] It modernizes Leo Tolstoy's parable of the same title. In both stories, three questions are posed that directly apply to fidelity. Those questions are:

> *Who are the most important people?*
>
> *What is the most important time to do things?*
>
> *What is the most important thing to do?*

Fidelity means discerning the most important commitments of time, energy, and resources to those in front of you. This is critical in a culture where people and things overwhelm and demand our attention. In any given hour, your most important commitment may be your job; another hour, your children, spouse, or a stranger.

One weekend while camping, I observed a midlife grandma who was raising her grandchildren. She wrangled two toddlers, making wisecracks about how doing such things surely would get her into heaven. Then she seamlessly soothed a sobbing two-year-old, put her down for a nap, then took the four-year-old fishing. This was a woman living out fidelity, doing hard things because they were the right things.

SCRIPTURE APPLICATION

Galatians 5:6 says the only thing that really counts is faith expressing itself in love. This may be the simplest form of commitment and loyalty. Love looks different for each person in each situation. However, it should always reflect Jesus and the work of the Holy Spirit.

Love is patient, kind, not jealous, boastful, or proud. It is not self-seeking, does not dishonor others, is not easily angered, and does not keep records of wrongs. Love rejoices with the truth. Fidelity always protects, always trusts, always hopes, and always perseveres (1 Corinthians 13:4–7).

The fidelity of Scripture is challenging. My dad did something difficult by standing up to a dishonest boss. Ellen did a hard thing by remaining true to her vows. Jillian was challenged caring for a mother who abandoned her. She said she doesn't regret spending that time with her mom; doing so even impacted her own healing. Faithfulness as an expression of love—of others and of God—can be its own fulfilling reward.

LET GO OF OUTGROWN COMMITMENTS

They say you put your money where your mouth is, but you also put time where your priorities are. To some, time is the litmus test for loyalty. It is a limited resource, so we need discernment to determine how best to use it.

In *Balance, Busyness, and Not Doing It All,* I encourage moms to prioritize what is most important during the busy years of parenting. Priorities ebb and flow in each season of your life. You will likely need to trade off certain responsibilities and commitments when they are no longer compatible with your life stage. I call it right-sizing your life, looking at who and what is most important to you in your season.

Each hour we spend doing one thing is another hour we are not doing something else. When the children were home, I wrote for different blogs, managed a few Facebook pages, and wrote a monthly mental health column in our local paper. Each activity took a few hours each week or month outside of my day job.

When the kids left home for college and jobs, I was overwhelmed trying to meet those writing deadlines on top of a new school job, traveling to visit the kids, or being available when they came home. I needed to right-size my life. I resigned from each writing responsibility, including the mental health column, because they no longer fit the priorities of my changing family and a new job.

I felt like I was disappointing people when I let go of those commitments. Some people may not understand your priorities when you say *no* or *not now*. They won't see things through your lens or know your answers to the Three Questions. I needed to focus on the most important duties in my life stage and not try to please others.

Finally, consider the drain social media and technology have on your time. Each minute you are online is a minute away from who and what is most important. Some online connections may be fulfilling and rich. However, try to be present with those around you by putting your phone down when in person with others. And when you're not, consider how your technology use at that moment benefits you and what it prevents you from doing. Sometimes, using technology is life-giving. Other times, it's life-giving to disconnect and use your time better elsewhere.

CULTIVATE FIDELITY

I often went to garage sales when my children were young. On one occasion, I picked up a vase from a box marked "free" after paying for my purchases. While driving away, my toddler said, "Mom, you shouldn't have stolen that."

I tried explaining the concept of "free," but they still did not understand. They could not reconcile that what I did was okay. I had taught them not to take things without paying or asking first. At that moment, though I was innocent, the most important person was my toddler and their young perception of right and wrong. The most important time was right then, teaching them at the level they understood. The most important thing to do was that which was right in their eyes.

I turned the car around, returned the vase, and explained the situation to the former owner. It was a lesson in fidelity I won't forget. Our actions look different from another's perspective. Tolstoy's questions inform situations that may be small to us but significant to another.

As you start living what's most important at the right time and doing what's best for the most important people before you, you'll leave indelible impressions on others. You'll be an unsung hero in your community, neighborhoods, family, and with strangers. People will recognize *that something* they want more of—fidelity.

SIMPLE SECRETS: NEXT STEPS

Now it's your turn. Here are simple suggestions to practice fidelity and uncomplicate your life:

- Send an encouraging text once a week to those most important to you.
- Make one intentional "a *said* is a *said*" you can follow through on. Ideas include a special activity with your child or grandchild or a date with a friend.

- Show up for a church, school, or community activity that needs volunteers.
- Take inventory of your activities, asking yourself if they fit your season of life.
- Attend an event that is important to a friend or family member.
- Turn off your phone or set it aside during the hours you are with your family. Or set a timer to check social media or emails a few times daily.
- Do one thing daily to deepen your most important relationships. Tell your spouse or child one thing about them you are grateful for. Text someone to see how they are doing.
- Pray for someone, then tell them that you are doing so.
- Replace a time-draining habit with one that makes a positive impact on others.

Prayer pause: *Invite Jesus to reveal what he desires for you from this chapter.*

REFLECTION

1. Ask yourself the Three Questions for your stage of life:
   Who are the most important people?
   What is the most important time to do things?
   What is the most important thing to do?
2. Who in your life exemplifies fidelity? How would you like to emulate them?
3. What did you learn from this chapter that is most helpful, or what reflects your needs and hopes? How will you apply it to your life?
4. What is one lesson of fidelity from your life that you can retell to another person?

Chapter 6

Calm, Cool, and Collected

To handle yourself, use your head; to handle others, use your heart.

—Eleanor Roosevelt[1]

Our son and daughter-in-law, Mark and Samantha, had purchased a remodeled farmhouse, and I was there cleaning before they moved in. Samantha was out getting several boxes at their old home a few miles away. My phone rang, and an unfamiliar number appeared on the screen.

Hesitantly, I answered it. "Hello, Brenda. This is John. There's been an accident in the woods, and a tree hit Ron." Fear gripped me. After teaching for thirty-two years, Ron retired and had just started driving for an Amish logging company. I prayed daily that God would keep him safe as he drove a truck and trailer around the state, pulling equipment or logs.

John's call was my worst fear. I asked questions to discern Ron's condition and what had happened. John answered with what information he knew. Then he reported they were airlifting Ron to the local trauma center. I panicked.

I imagined the worst-case scenarios. I got ready to drive to the hospital, which was over an hour away, realizing I needed to call our four kids who lived away from home. Ethan was in college, Mark was teaching, Jenna was working in another state, and Drew had recently moved to Oklahoma. The last thing they needed was to receive news about their dad from a hysterical mom. I needed equanimity.

I took a deep breath and paused. I thought about helpful strategies I use when working with others in crises. I needed to focus on what I knew rather than speculating about unknowns. I called Samantha first since she needed to know I was leaving. Her calm response mirrored what the other kids needed from me. I then called each child, one by one, reporting what I knew. "Being airlifted to a trauma center is precautionary for most head injuries," I told them. We would know more when I arrived at the hospital.

Driving to the trauma center, I was fearful. I focused on the road ahead, listening to the rhythm of the windshield wipers in the rain. I asked God to calm me, get me there safely, and help me with the unknowns.

WHEN LIFE FALLS APART

Most of us have probably experienced that phone call, conversation, or text message that turns a stable and predictable world upside down. Emotions flood your thoughts with fear and panic. Being calm is the last thing you think you are capable of.

Twenty years before, Ron and I had a similar experience when Ron's mom unexpectedly died from a blood clot in her lung after an outpatient surgery. I felt like I heard glass shatter when the hospital chaplain told us she had expired. Everything I knew about life and God seemed to break apart simultaneously. I had to return to reality, focusing on what I knew was certain and true.

The scene felt familiar when I arrived at the trauma center. The emergency room doctor said it was a miracle that Ron did not have life-altering injuries, even that he was alive at all. He suffered from multiple injuries, including open head wounds, which I watched them staple closed on the back of his head. It wasn't until I crawled into bed the night of the accident that the weight of the event hit me. I was grateful God gave me the composure to be present for Ron and the kids when they needed me rather than being overcome by panic.

FORBEARANCE AND EQUANIMITY: THE SIXTH SECRET

Equanimity—part of the sixth secret—is the possession of mental calmness, composure, and an even temper, especially in difficult situations. It is not my natural tendency, as it is Ron's. I have honed it professionally as a classroom teacher and therapist, but I'm continuously working on it in my family life.

Ron and I often clashed when experiencing conflicts early in our relationship. Emotions, words, and reactions were freely expressed in my family of origin, so this felt more natural to me. Not to him. Growing up on a farm, Ron learned the essential skills of restraint, forbearance, and being even-tempered. Things go wrong, but getting angry doesn't help. Animals die, but sadness and disappointment can't dictate daily responsibilities. Ron knew you couldn't control outcomes on the farm, but you could control how you reacted to frustrating and challenging situations.

Meanwhile, my formative years were shaped by fighting disordered eating. Big emotions drove extreme behaviors as

I calmed and controlled my feelings with starvation or over-eating, then purging. Even though I mastered weight and food issues as an adult, I didn't learn healthy replacement strategies for big feelings or hurt for several years. I often overreacted with intense words and feelings, which landed on Ron and the kids.

Perhaps you struggle with extreme thoughts or reactions to big emotions. They're almost expected today. Civil public discourse seems to have vanished. Many of us need better modeling of responding calmly to offenses, disruptions, or adverse experiences. Two long-forgotten skills—forbearance and equanimity—will help us. Let's get reacquainted with them.

CALM AND COOL

Forbearance—the other part of the sixth secret—is patient self-control, restraint, and tolerance. Equanimity is its worthy companion, with that even-mindedness and calm composure. I could use more familiar terms such as self-control and balance, but neither encompasses the breadth of meaning as do their old-fashioned counterparts.

We witness forbearance and equanimity more in the workplace than in our homes. We bring our best selves to work because lack of restraint has professional consequences. Home is where we live unbridled. Often parents don't understand why their child is well-behaved at school but more emotional or out of control at home. It's because home is where we feel safe and let down our guard.

Yet, it wasn't always this way. Daily life in past generations was difficult and required an even temperament. Making breakfast entailed rising early, starting a cookstove with firewood, milking a cow, gathering eggs, and cutting ham off the cured hog hanging in the smokehouse. I'm sure my great-grandmother, with fourteen children, woke up in a bad mood some mornings if she got any sleep at all. But she couldn't dwell on it. Remaining calm for the daily responsibilities was expected and practiced.

Likewise, the night Ron's mom died, he still awoke at 2:00 a.m. to milk cows. Familiar rhythms help us in times of uncertainty and chaos. That calm composure of forbearance and equanimity helps us in all areas of disruptions.

LITTLE EYES WATCH

A few years ago, Ron looked out the kitchen window while the kids ate breakfast. He noticed our four-wheel ATV was not in front of the barn where he had parked it the night before. He asked each of our sons if they had moved it. They all said no.

He stood at the window, quiet, getting a drink of water. Then he said, "It must have been stolen." There was silence in the kitchen as I observed three kids watching their dad. The pause of prudence hung in the air. Ron didn't react but said, "There's not much I can do." He called the police to make a report. Based on the tire impressions the police found, the culprits silenced our guard dogs between midnight and 6:00 a.m., rolled the ATV through a flower bed, and onto a trailer by the road.

Ron called the insurance company and continued his day. His measured response was one of those ordinary moments that make an impression on others. His calm control made a powerful statement to the kids and me.

Our actions impact others, especially when we are parenting. As a young mom, I was a reactive parent, the opposite of Ron. They say what is caught is more important than what is taught. It's true. If you struggle with volatile reactions to situations, you're not alone. You also don't have to remain in those patterns. When I realized the weight of my actions on

my kids as they grew older, I was prompted to seek the change
I needed.

THE POWER SOURCE

God doesn't leave us to develop equanimity and forbearance
alone. The attributes are embedded in the fruit of the Holy
Spirit—peace, patience, gentleness, kindness, and self-control
(Galatians 5:22–23). These qualities are byproducts of God's
transformation in us. We should not feel shame or guilt when
these don't come naturally. All people experience anger, fear,
and other big feelings. What we do with them is what matters.
It's easier to develop self-control, patience, and mental calmness when we have the assistance of the Holy Spirit. Yielding
our will to God changes us.

This happens through a personal relationship with Jesus
Christ. You can communicate as directly with him as you do
with others you have a relationship with. Prayer is the way we
talk to God. Reading the Bible is God's way of speaking to and
refining us. Reflective listening is another practice that helps us
hear what God may have to say to us. And it's an important
one—we often pray or talk to God without pausing to listen
and hear what the Holy Spirit may be speaking to our hearts.

IT DOESN'T HAPPEN OVERNIGHT

My friend Shannon and I were having lunch, discussing the
counseling careers we were both entering in midlife. We were
also childhood acquaintances reconnecting. She shared that
her calling to the counseling profession grew from her sobriety
journey. She correlated it to the eating disorder she knew I had
struggled with for years. She then said something that brought
me to tears. "Brenda, you've done such hard work overcoming
an eating disorder. That's a big deal."

She was the first person in my life who acknowledged and validated the hard work of overcoming disordered eating. I worked for years to develop self-control and equanimity with food, body image, and distorted thinking. It's internal work that few people see, let alone speak out loud. Perhaps you have experienced similar unseen growth.

Self-control, tolerance, and even-mindedness are essential for healthy lifestyles and relationships. When your brain and body are regulated, you are calm. The more calming strategies you use when your body is distressed, the more rationally you can respond. They activate your brain to create new patterns for thoughts and behaviors. These happened to me over time by practicing self-control and restraint, such as refraining from the urge to binge or walking away from an argument when I was tempted to explode with angry words.

Forbearance and equanimity are not lost arts. They are cultivated. The better you can control your emotions, thoughts, and reactions, the easier it is to handle those things that rock our world. Which, today, is a lot.

IT'S EVERYWHERE

Living in Amish country doesn't remove me or others from the polarized and enraged culture that surrounds us. With each mass shooting and fear-based headline, an edginess finds its way into our conversations and sense of security. These things have socialized an entire generation.

Working in a public school exposes me to a cross-section of needs that occur in all communities. I have worked in city, suburban, and rural schools—no location is immune from violence, racism, abuse, addiction, or lack of restraint. The more self-control, mental calmness, and self-discipline we employ in our environments, the more attractive and powerful these virtues are in contrast to our culture's alternatives. We need to see, feel, and touch *that something*, because its archenemy is easier to feed with immediate rewards that are actually destructive.

Just as prudence's pause requires effort, so too does self-restraint. Our flesh really desires to do whatever it wants. Yet we crave moderation. God created us for order, not chaos. *We can do anything, but not everything is beneficial.*

A NEW MINDSET

I don't remember what Drew said that upset me as we sat on the couch, but I remember his eyes after I scolded him. It was the first time I directly noticed how my reactions affected my kids. We don't recognize unhealthy patterns when we are immersed in them. They are familiar to us, like that old sweatshirt that's smelly and stained, but you wear it because it's comfortable and has been with you. It doesn't judge you.

Our unharnessed thoughts, feelings, and behaviors are similar. They are comfortable and have been part of us. We don't see how ugly they are until we have outgrown the behaviors and see them in a different light. Drew's facial response was a mirror of my years of overreacting. The experience helped me realize how my undisciplined words and tone affected our family.

A mindset of forbearance and equanimity is cultivated by controlling one thought, feeling, and action at a time. It is challenging, though, when we are used to succumbing to impulsivity and mindlessness. Dysregulated thoughts, feelings, and actions burden much of our lives and relationships. Healthier internal systems uncomplicate our lives and relationships, creating a more peaceful and even-minded presence within ourselves.

Something that has helped me is changing fatalistic thoughts to more moderate ones. Do you commonly say words like *all, nothing, everything, everyone, all the time, always,* or *never*?

These are red flags for big feelings ready to erupt. You may even say, "You *never* listen!"; "I'll *never* be good enough!"; or "You do that *all the time*!" Polarizing words like these reflect something in our hearts that needs to be heard, remedied, or healed.

You can temper these thoughts by recognizing the red flag words. Pause, and even write them down if you can. Then ask yourself whether the statement is true or not (usually it is not). Identify your feelings behind the statement, then reframe the statement by writing or restating what is true. Instead of saying, "You do that all the time," what's true may be that the person interrupts you sometimes. But when they do, you feel discounted and unheard.

When red flag words arise, be curious about their origin. It usually indicates an underlying narrative or wound that you may need to address.

CLEAN AND SORT

I was cleaning out Ethan's childhood bedroom after he married. As I cleaned and sorted what he left behind, God used the process to help me grow forbearance and equanimity.

I was anxious and irritated that day because a few relationship wounds had surfaced. Sometimes, out of nowhere, the hurt arises. As I cleaned, a flood of past thoughts and anxiety reappeared. Those red flag words and big feelings pinged between my head and heart.

As I sorted Ethan's items, I considered the value of holding on to different things. The Holy Spirit invited me to ask the same questions about those relationship wounds. Why was I holding on to feelings and outcomes I couldn't control? Was it helpful to cling to hurt and bitterness? The cleaning and sorting ritual wasn't just about housekeeping that day. I learned there's a time to keep certain things and time for others, like hurt and disappointments, to be let go.

SCRIPTURE APPLICATION

Ecclesiastes 3:1–8 provides a beautiful example of forbearance and equanimity. There is a time for everything and a season for every activity. This is what farmers witness within the cycle of life. There's a time to be born and a time to die. A time to tear down and build up. A time to embrace and refrain from embracing. A time to be silent and a time to speak. A time to weep. A time to keep and a time to throw away.

The rhythm is the concept of *both/and*. It's God's order for life. He created us with the ability to accommodate opposing experiences, like birth and death, sometimes within the same day. Big feelings are typical. Equanimity engages our frontal lobe—the brain's logic center—to talk to our amygdala—the brain's feeling center—letting it know there is space to feel happy *and* sad, anger *and* joy, disappointment *and* fondness. These uncomfortable paradoxes can coexist—sometimes we must remind ourselves of this truth.

My coworker says that rather than being bothered by what she can't control, she focuses on what she can. I have seen her apply this with students in crises but also with significant personal events, like a parent receiving a devastating diagnosis. Most circumstances in daily life are routine until something big happens you weren't anticipating. When it does, it can blindside you or make you feel unstable when just a few minutes before life felt certain and secure. Rather than allowing overwhelming circumstances to control you and your life's outlook, you can feel more in control when you release what you can't. Then, with prudence, you focus on what you can: thoughts, feelings, and actions.

The fruit of the Spirit provides freedom from things that can bind us to circumstances. My transformation from disordered eating and uncontrolled reactions began with asking the Holy Spirit to give me self-control and seeking God through prayer, Bible reading, and accountability. When words I said hurt someone, I asked for forgiveness. 1 John 1:9 says that when we confess our sins, God is faithful and just to forgive our sins and purify us from all unrighteousness.

Talking about sin is not politically correct. But it was never and should not be political. It's a heart condition in relationship to God and others. I cannot master forbearance and equanimity on my own—neither can you. Human nature is too selfish. Instead, accepting Jesus' restorative work on the cross allows him to transform what you and I cannot. His presence then fills us with love, joy, peace, patience, kindness, goodness, gentleness, faithfulness, and self-control.

A LIFESTYLE OF FORBEARANCE AND EQUANIMITY

I've witnessed Mara face multiple disappointments and losses with equanimity and forbearance. These include infertility, failed adoptions, and both of her parents dying by her early thirties. She attributes her mental calmness in difficult situations to the same mindset my coworker engages: she can only respond to what she can control. If her emotions rule her, she can't think and respond clearly, a skill she needs as an ICU nurse. She remains calm in crises by relaxing her shoulders and taking deep breaths. Whether at work or at home, she sets aside time to process her thoughts and emotions, sometimes by setting a timer so she returns her mind to the tasks at hand when it goes off.

Similarly, my friend Leigh has experienced multiple losses with stillborn babies. I witnessed how she allowed herself to grieve with each loss. It would have been tempting to let each one destroy her capacity to move forward and parent her living children. I saw her instead cling to God's presence in her pain and grief. She did not rush through her lament as part of her healing process. She also had consistent routines as a working farmer, getting up each morning to milk cows. Being among nature's rhythms of life and death grounded her hope and sustained her peace.

Tending to your feelings during loss, change, or life transitions is important. This may look like seeing a counselor, attending a grief group, or going on a short trip to refresh and be in a different environment. Or it may look like incorporating new rhythms in your routine, such as morning meditations, walking, working through a self-help book, or other activities that foster your healing.

Many cultures have traditions that foster lament in times of mourning. Emotional expressions that engage your whole self in sorrow, joy, or celebration have multiple benefits. Outward expressions of internal feelings such as grief or excitement acknowledge and validate such emotions and the meaning attached to them. Often these experiences happen in community where love and support are expressed and received. Such cultural traditions teach us healthy processes for life's experiences.

In contrast, some cultures or family systems avoid or suppress emotions. This can send messages of condemnation, judgment, or shame when strong feelings arise. Emotions are God's natural processes and shouldn't be judged—by ourselves or others. When I hear people apologize for crying, I tell them it's okay to cry. We need to give each other permission to appropriately feel and process loss and general feelings so they are not buried inside, where they may eventually erupt or be misplaced upon others.

LET GO OF HABITS AND HURTS

Habits and hurts have a natural relationship. Both inform our thoughts and feelings and can harm and hinder our health. Releasing them creates freedom, peace, and a disciplined life. Ridding yourself of blame—whether for bad habits you have developed or hurts you have absorbed—also frees you to be responsible for your current behavior and what you can change.

In his later years, my father shared with me about the volatile household he grew up in and his father's harshness, though he didn't disclose many details. The more I learned, the more I respected my dad's self-control and equanimity during my own growing-up years. I rarely saw him angry.

The year before his death, I thanked Dad for his gentleness as a father, asking him how he fostered that, since he didn't have it modeled for him as a child. He said that when he left home as an adult, he vowed to himself that he wouldn't be like his dad. My father didn't go to therapy—few people did back then—but he learned to use his God-given ability to have self-control, even mindedness, and restraint. He also let go of hurt and blame.

Similarly, when you and I let go of hurt, blame, and shame, we are more able to control big emotions. For years I thought something was inherently wrong with me because I was passionate and more emotional than others. I stuffed and starved myself to silence and shrink everything about me. I could better accept how God created me when I finally allowed the Holy Spirit to transform my thoughts, feelings, and actions.

Naming your feelings is one of the most helpful ways to manage them. Listen to your body, head, and heart. Be curious about how you feel. Let go of the mindset that feelings are bad. The less afraid you are of your emotions, the more they help you learn what's behind them.

Perhaps you struggle with self-acceptance, shame, or judgment. Shame is different from restorative guilt. The latter helps us identify when we have done something wrong or need to change. The former is a negative identity someone puts on you, such as, "Shame on you!" Shame and blame are not who you are. Take off that familiar stained sweatshirt and let it go.

CULTIVATE FORBEARANCE AND EQUANIMITY

I was teaching a lesson at school when I was handed a note from the office. There had been a local tragedy, and counselors were asked to assist.

I felt ill-equipped to respond. Nothing prepares you for tragic events, even when you are trained in best practices. Then God reminded me that I had just been through a different kind of tragedy with Ron's accident. If I could have equanimity for my children, I could do something similar for someone else's child now.

As Ecclesiastes 3 says, you and I will experience everything under the heavens—adversity, disappointment, death, and pain. God has designed a beautiful process between our brain and body to handle whatever life gives us. His presence, through the Holy Spirit, provides divine qualities we cannot manifest without him. As we allow the fruit of the Spirit to flourish in our lives, we will become the calm presence of self-control and balance that our families and communities need.

I've witnessed this in my friend, Janiya. Being even-minded helped sustain her growing up in a home with mental illness and chaos. Her experience also provided her with empathy and insight into differing perspectives. I have seen her have self-control and a healthy tolerance for complex situations. When faced with multiple losses in her adult life, she has walked through them with perseverance, hope, and an honest faith that God is with her.

Psalm 16:6–8 says, "The boundary lines have fallen for me in pleasant places; surely I have a delightful inheritance. I will praise the LORD, who counsels me. . . . With him at my right hand, I will not be shaken." Safety, security, and freedom can be found within the boundaries God places in our lives.

What we journey through will often be hard. Walking with God, listening to his counsel, and abiding in his presence equips us with forbearance and equanimity to say, "I will not be shaken."

SIMPLE SECRETS: NEXT STEPS

Now it's your turn. Here are simple suggestions to practice equanimity and forbearance to help uncomplicate your life.

- Pray through the fruits of the Spirit in Galatians 5:22–23. Focus on applying one attribute throughout the day.
- Create a list of activities that calm you. Doing puzzles, coloring, working with your hands, listening to music—the list can be endless!
- Identify what you can control and what is out of your control. Then focus on what you can do to have healthy responses, thoughts, and actions.
- Drink a glass of water when you feel out of control. Water hydrates the brain and calms your body.
- Pay attention to red flag thoughts (always, never, etc.). Think about a more rational statement. Write the

distorted thought down, then write a corresponding statement of positive truth.

- Learn mindfulness techniques. Choose one that helps you and practice it daily.
- Create a calming toolkit with items that calm you down. It may be a coloring book, listening to music, or watching a calming YouTube video.
- Be aware of how your body responds to stressful situations. Pause to ask yourself why your heart is racing, you have a headache, or you feel anxious.
- Look around a room when you feel out of control. Pause to name five things you see, four things you feel, three things you hear, two things you smell, and one thing you taste.
- Print a feelings wheel to keep handy when you are dysregulated so you can identify specific emotions.
- Seek professional help if needed.

Prayer pause: *Invite Jesus to reveal what he desires for you from this chapter.*

REFLECTION

1. What areas of forbearance or equanimity are you prompted to grow after reading this chapter?
2. Who in your life exemplifies forbearance and equanimity? How would you like to emulate them?
3. What did you learn that is most helpful, or what reflects your needs and hopes in this chapter? How can you apply this to your life?
4. What is one lesson of forbearance or equanimity from your life that you can retell to another person?

Chapter 7

Brighten the Corner Where You Are

If I can do some good today, Lord, show me how.
—Grenville Kleiser[1]

Our doorbell rang early one evening. It was one of the first summers we lived near the farm, and the kids were inside playing. Ron had just come home from milking and was cleaning up.

A young man was at the door when I answered it. He asked if he could use the phone to call someone to give him a ride. He told me he had walked from a homeless shelter over twenty-five miles away in a larger city. He was walking to his home of origin several miles east of us.

Having a stranger stop by in need was not a new experience for Ron growing up in his parents' farmhouse. Strangers often stopped for various reasons: a car out of gas, someone needing directions, or various circumstances. I had seen Ron's mom and dad respond with generosity and charity on all occasions. Never had I seen them turn away someone in need. But for me, this was the first time someone came to *our* home shortly after we moved near the family farm.

With prudence, I asked the man to remain on the front porch while I got Ron and the phone. Ron stepped onto the porch with our phone and started chatting with the guest. I went about my work making supper and corralling the kids as ten minutes turned into thirty, then sixty. I peeked out the window and saw Ron and the man sitting on the porch stoop talking.

Dinnertime came and went. Ron and the man were still outside. It was getting close to dusk. Knowing they were probably hungry, I made two plates of food and brought them outside. They ate. As it got darker, it was evident the man's ride was not coming.

Not knowing what to do next, we asked the man if we could call our local police to see if they could take him to a safe location for the night. The man agreed and was soon picked up.

When I think of this experience, Hebrews 13:2 comes to mind. It says, "Do not forget to show hospitality to strangers, for by doing so some people have shown hospitality to angels without knowing it."

I never considered the man an angel, but Ron and I both felt *that something* that was sacred from the experience. Whether it's a stranger at your door, your family, a neighbor, or an animal, God calls us to steward those he puts in our care. It is a quality that permeates my local community and is an important part of an uncomplicated life.

CONNECTED AND CARED FOR

Our rural Amish and Mennonite community has its own unique version of "Midwest nice." Tourists have remarked that people seem to go out of their way for one another. Upon moving back to the community from a suburban area, my nephew's wife noted, "People see you here. They know if something is wrong and help." It's just how we do things.

We can do this for each other no matter where we live. When I spoke at a MOPS (Mothers of Preschoolers) group in a large suburban church a few years ago, several moms remarked how lonely they were, living far from their extended families and parents. But, they said, the MOPS peers and the mentor moms in the group had become like family to them. When they had needs and felt alone, they had a community of people to assist them.

To be cared for and connected is *that something* many of us need, whether married or single, with kids at home, in midlife, or older. When talking to midlife moms about the topics in *Fledge: Launching Your Kids Without Losing Your Mind*, many women report feeling lonely and disconnected because they don't have a full house anymore. Living with family is a built-in community that quickly vanishes with an empty nest.

In my role as a school counselor, I encounter many families that don't have a community of support outside of themselves. Often families seeking help or in crisis call their child's school because they don't know where else to turn. Most often, parents just need a listening ear and compassionate conversation.

Humans are not created for isolation. We feel loved, cared for, and understood when others see and meet our needs. In contrast, lack of support and community can breed problems for many people, even affecting our mental health. Struggles can feel bigger when we are overwhelmed and alone. As the body of Christ, God calls us to see, steward, and respond to his creation and everything in it.

STEWARDSHIP: THE SEVENTH SECRET

What does stewardship, our seventh secret, entail? 1 Corinthians 4:2 (NKJV) says it is required of stewards to be found faithful. A steward of something or someone is guided by responsibility and accountability for what is entrusted to their care, now and in the future. Stewards nurture and protect rather than harm and exploit.

Stewardship is a sacred calling we should handle with careful intention. We each have stewardship responsibilities within our personal and professional lives. We have been entrusted to care for and manage all God has created and given us.

The Mennonite Confession of Faith[2] includes stewardship in its tenets, reflecting a belief that we are made for a relationship with God; because of that, we are to steward all he has created, acknowledging God's ownership of all things. This includes living at peace with one another and caring for the rest of creation. Because of this theological emphasis, Mennonites and the Amish have a strong heritage of caring for others and stewarding the land. We corporately practice disaster relief, voluntary service, environmental stewardship, community service, and hospitality.

But stewardship is not exclusive to the Amish and Mennonites. All Christians are called to steward people and nature through how we use our time, talents, and treasures. You may not consider yourself a steward of anything outside your finances, family, or environment. Or you may think stewardship responsibilities belong to rural life. Farmers are often called stewards of the land—managing, nurturing, and caring for their animals and soil. But God puts all of us in circles of influence to care for those around us.

ICE, ICE BABY

Ron had never seen the creek behind our house freeze so solid that he could walk across it, but this day it had. It was dangerous for the cattle—they would be unable to get water to drink on a blustery winter day. I was cozy in the house with coffee, but he went outside in the below-zero windchills and snowdrifts to ensure his animals had what they needed.

This is the nature of rural stewardship. You check on your animals just as you do your family. You get up in the middle of the night when one is birthing. You notice when something is wrong and get them help. Even if you don't live on a farm, you also are such a steward when you respond to needs around you—checking on your neighbor, caring for your pets, or even tending the plants on your windowsill.

God calls us to steward those within our care, especially those near us; our spouses, children, grandchildren, and parents; those we mentor, shepherd, or teach. Sometimes we selfishly want to steward only those closest to us. But I like to think of stewardship as hospitality on the go—that caring, welcoming spirit that goes with you to be extended to those who cross your path.

The Good Samaritan parable in Luke 10:25–37 is a great example of hospitality and stewardship outside our familiar circles. In it, Jesus tells of a man robbed, beaten, and left for dead. Two religious leaders walked by him, ignoring his condition. Then a Samaritan, who was culturally looked down upon by the first-century Jews, tended to the man's wounds and got him to safety. Jesus said the one who showed mercy was a neighbor to the man. Jesus commands us to do likewise.

THROW LOVE AROUND LIKE CONFETTI

Hospitality is often considered something you do within your home when entertaining or having guests. It's that, but much more. It's treating guests and strangers warmly and generously no matter where we are. As the song says, people should know we are Christians by our love.

A Bob Goff quote is taped on my kitchen cabinet so I can read it daily: "Don't save up love like you're trying to retire on it. Give it away like you're made of it."[3] It helps me think of generosity and hospitality as inherited wealth to give away. Except it costs nothing! And it's desperately needed. Have you looked at others around you? Humankind is struggling. Our communities need the love of Christ, and they need it now.

Isaiah 49:1 says that before we were born, God called us. Before our births, he made mention of our names. Isn't that incredible? God knows each person and cares about us. There is no discrimination of any kind by the Creator. All need and deserve the love of Christ.

This means that Christian hospitality is more than polite conversation. It's the living, breathing, warm glow of the Holy Spirit's presence that says, "Welcome, you are safe here." It's the example I've seen modeled numerous times by compelling individuals who help and care for others whenever possible, regardless of gender, social-economic status, race, sexual orientation, age, or morality. Every person is made in God's image and deserves honor. As actress and children's rights advocate Audrey Hepburn said, "Never throw anyone out."[4]

When teaching a fourth-grade lesson, I once asked students to identify three of their strengths. One student caught my attention when the strength he wrote was "going broke." I stopped and asked the student what he meant by that. He said, "I give things away to people who don't have any." It reminded me how uncomplicated stewardship is and how much it's needed. Jesus says we are to have faith like a little child. I want to be like that student.

AM I MY BROTHER'S KEEPER?

Stewardship has a tension, though. We can't solve all the world's problems. So how do we not turn inward and become callous toward others? Genesis records the consequences of apathy, malice, and self-protection when Cain kills his brother Abel. When God asks him for his brother's whereabouts, Cain responds in Genesis 4:9, "Am I my brother's keeper?"

I can hear our generation asking the same question. While we say God is love and speak about loving others, violence in all forms abounds. Callousness, self-protection, and malice are not new, as Galatians 5:19–21 reminds us: "The acts of the flesh are obvious . . . hatred, discord, jealousy, fits of rage, selfish ambition, dissensions, factions, and envy; drunkenness, orgies, and the like."

Humanity's worst behavior toward others now has new places to go through online platforms. We see this through the rise of child pornography, human trafficking, and the negative effects of social media. Social psychologist Jonathan Haidt writes about the causation between the rise of social media and epidemic depression and anxiety in youth, especially girls.[5] When social media replaces natural socialization, unhealthy beliefs and behaviors are internalized and processed in a vacuum. Human connection, in contrast, helps someone make meaning from troubling experiences. The physical presence of a caring person fosters a protective buffer from society's increasingly dark side.

God's sobering standard for humanity's stewardship—especially children and the vulnerable—is seen in Matthew 18:6.

It says that if anyone causes a child to stumble, it would be better for them to have a large millstone hung around their neck and drown in the depths of the sea. God calls us toward this powerful protective care. It goes beyond just preventing harm it is a spiritual shield that encircles children and others.

I see a tangible example of this when babies are dedicated in Ron's home congregation. Traditionally, the pastor carries a baby or toddler down the aisle of the sanctuary after the congregation reads a collective commitment to protectively nurture that child's growth and development. The practice is a visual reminder of the responsibility we are charged with as humankind's keepers.

God designed it so that each positive interaction we have with someone makes a powerful difference in their lives. Stewardship doesn't involve rescuing the world—it's simply being faithful with our presence in the life of another. Studies show that simple eye contact—and a smile—releases oxytocin, the bonding hormone, in someone's brain, even a stranger. This creates the attachment we need through a human connection that tells us we are valued and seen, even if for a moment. Let's see how to grow such a powerful mindset.

A NEW MINDSET

I was driving to a speaking event when a woman walking on the side of the highway caught my eye. She had a small backpack and was briskly walking away from a semi pulled over on the side of the road. The driver's side door was open, and a man got out and followed the woman. I noticed in the review mirror that she kept looking behind her and increasing her pace. Something in my gut warned me that the woman might have been in danger.

I pulled several yards ahead and watched in my rearview mirror as the woman neared my car. I am trained in abuse response and educated about human trafficking. Various scenarios played out in my mind about the situation, including potential danger to me if I helped.

But stewards protect. I could not turn a blind eye to a potentially harmful situation for someone who may need help. Prudence made me pause to consider the safest way to respond. Prayer followed. As the woman approached my locked car, I rolled down my window partway and asked if she needed help. She paused, answering no, saying she was walking to Ohio, just a few miles from our location. I asked her if she was sure. Her eyes met mine. She paused, said yes, thanking me for my concern.

Driving away, I continued to be concerned for her as I saw the semi still parked in its position. I pulled over on the next crossroad, called 911, and asked for a welfare check sharing the woman's location. The dispatcher reported that he would send an officer to check on her.

You may think, "I'd never do that; it's too dangerous!" You're right. It was dangerous. Depending on your situation and training, it may have been too dangerous for you to do the same thing. Each of us must have a mindset for stewardship that is willing to help but also assess the unpredictable situations we may find ourselves in. God's call to protect looks different for each of us. He has a particular reason for putting us in our daily environments, and you may be uniquely equipped to handle the challenges that come your way.

You may have a call to steward animals, like Ron's mom. Lois rescued several abandoned or hurt animals when Ron was growing up. Or you may be like Annie, my colleague, who deeply cares for the earth. She started a recycling program at our school that makes an incredible difference in the amount of paper that would otherwise go in the trash. It also teaches a mindset of environmental stewardship to over four hundred children.

God has placed an environment around you to steward. You may not see it or think that it matters. Begin believing it does. Train your eyes, thoughts, and heart to see what God may be asking you to care for. It may be investing in those around you, in new or different ways. Or, it may be having a new perspective of stewarding the most ordinary moments.

SMALL ACTS

One summer when Ethan was in grade school, I took him on a day trip to Chicago. We walked up and down the Magnificent Mile, often passing homeless individuals. Ethan was bothered by the fact that we passed them without helping them. One person had a sign that read, "I'm hungry."

"Mom," he said. "We need to help them." An ordinary, big moment presented itself. I needed to steward Ethan's moral development and reject the callousness often felt in response to bigger-than-yourself problems.

I took Ethan to a street vendor a few yards from where we were. We purchased a sandwich and drink with the small cash I had with me. We took the food to the person with the sign, hoping to meet their immediate need.

Society's needs feel overwhelming at times. We may all have different ideas about how to address the problems. You may think my way of doing so is mistaken. That's okay. Most importantly, we should ask the Three Questions when we encounter a Samaritan situation. *Who are the most important people in front of me right now? What is the most important time to respond? What is the most important thing to do?*

Austrian Holocaust survivor Viktor Frankl reminds us that we can either exist in our space or color it in with our presence and the good we can do within it.[6] When things feel overwhelming, my coworker Annie reminds me not to worry about what we can't control. Instead, do what we can to brighten our corner of the world. That perspective uncomplicates most things in life.

SCRIPTURE APPLICATION

Jesus is Scripture's blueprint for loving God by loving others through our actions and words. Romans 14:19 says, "Let us therefore make every effort to do what leads to peace and to mutual edification." What does this look like in real life?

Mutual edification is instructing or improving another person and allowing ourselves to receive the same from others, especially morally or spiritually. It builds another up. Like fidelity and interdependence, it urges us to seek a lifestyle of other-centeredness, not self-centeredness.

The story of the Good Samaritan tells us we are to love our neighbor as ourselves. Our neighbors are those in our spheres of influence. We are to welcome them, nurture them, and when they are in need, show mercy. A kind word, a small deed done, or even a conversation tends to a person's soul, even ours.

Our call to stewardship is extended beyond people. God cares about nature and the earth and calls us to do the same. Psalm 115:16 says the heavens are God's, but he has given humankind the earth. Stewardship of nature has been our calling since creation, well before environmental and political initiatives.

As a culture, we disconnected ourselves from responsibility to nature as populations moved from the farms to the cities. Consumerism and materialism replaced more agrarian values. If environmentalism or climate change are negative buzzwords words for you, reframe them in the context of stewardship. We care for all living things and protect what we can for future generations because it's the right thing to do as image bearers of Jesus Christ.

A STEWARDSHIP LIFESTYLE

The Colonel was a guest in our Airbnb suite whom we will not forget. He had traveled across the country to see his favorite singer perform at the Blue Gate Theater in Shipshewana. An eccentric older gentleman, he shared with us how a near-death experience gave him the resolve to care for anything that came across his path because of the grace God had given him.

The Colonel genuinely loved people and nature. While staying with us, he spent much time interacting with our animals and soaking up the nature around him. He left behind a written prayer for our property, praying God's blessing over those who come to rest and for the animals we raise.

Our interaction with him was a reminder of an uncomplicated lifestyle of stewardship. It showed me the powerful impact our resources have when we offer them to others. The Colonel's actions reminded me of a poem Ron's mom, Lois, kept in a prayer book that she had copied in her own handwriting. It's entitled "My Daily Prayer," and attributed to Grenville Kleiser. A repeated phrase in the poem is, "If I can do some good today, Lord show me how."[7] It lists simple acts such as helping another person smile or lightening their burden. It models a life of stewardship and hospitality, like that I witnessed in Lois's life.

My friend Scott is someone who also exemplifies this lifestyle. His young son died from a terminal illness, and he uses that experience to support families whose children are dying. He sits and listens to them, answering hard questions without trite answers. He uses his woodworking and artistic talents to make meaningful crafts and paintings for the hospitals and families he serves.

Good stewards employ their resources of time, talent, and treasures to make a difference in the lives of others. I could list the names of many who do it well. One teaches special education and doesn't give up on her students. One pours herself into our community's teens. Another helps her special needs child live to the highest capacity he can.

Good stewards care for others. As caregivers, we also must care for ourselves.

LET GO OF BURNOUT

You may be familiar with the term *self-care*, but it doesn't encompass the responsibility of stewardship. So I'm introducing you to the concept of *self-stewardship*. Caring for oneself is essential when caring for others, whether you're a parent, a helping professional, or a filial caregiver. It equips you to let go of burnout.

A book that first helped me think about caregiver stewardship was *Trauma Stewardship: An Everyday Guide to Caring for Self While Caring for Others*.[8] I came across it when I was depleted from providing trainings on how to respond to child abuse, domestic violence, and toxic marriages, while also counseling many in those situations. The book helped me understand that stewardship extends beyond just physical resources. It also means caring for and growing the callings in our lives, especially as that calling relates to others.

Because most caregiving relationships are not reciprocal, caregivers are often drained by the high demands, hours, and physical and emotional toll of caring for others. Tired and exhausted, we often don't speak up for our needs or delegate responsibilities to others. In turn we suffer, and those we care for suffer because we can't help others when we are not cared for.

Instead we need to set boundaries around us as a protective barrier of stewardship. This may mean saying "No" to responsibilities that are outside of work or our immediate families. It may be surrounding ourselves with encouraging friends, or delegating household chores. This also includes making time to do what fuels rather than drains you, like walking, gardening, or reading. My friend Mara, a critical care nurse and mom, sets time aside for herself to walk or enjoy nature. She also prioritizes time with like-minded friends to talk about parenting or nursing. These little practices fill her up and protect her against depletion.

Likewise, when my friend Dorie cared for her terminally ill husband, she struggled at first with caring for herself. She often felt compelled to use every moment with Randy intentionally. But her exhaustion told her differently; she needed to rest. She learned to listen to her body, mind, and heart for what she needed.

She also learned the importance of separating her roles as caregiver and wife. She told me, "You can lose your identity as a person and a spouse, both caregiving and taking on the responsibilities your spouse can no longer do. Sometimes you just need to sit quietly and be a wife, not the caregiver."

Stewarding yourself is hard for women, especially in Christian circles. We are socialized to serve others at all costs and then more—with a smile, a great attitude, and an extra apple pie in the oven. You are not alone if you struggle to set healthy boundaries for yourself. Let someone else help you—a mentor, coach, or counselor who can help you identify your needs, ease your mental and emotional burdens, and identify areas of growth or change. I'll share one way I learned to steward a caregiving profession while also parenting.

STEWARDING YOUR SEASON

When I first began counseling, I worked in both foster care and for a domestic violence agency. The work was raw. Exposure to secondary trauma affected my emotional availability for my own kids in junior high and high school.

I worked in this capacity for a few years until prudence told me that a work environment with better boundaries would be healthier for me while parenting. I only had my children to steward for a short season—I needed to better care for them and myself. I took a counseling position in an intermediate school, which provided the right balance for several years.

Your stewardship circle has different dilemmas. You may be knee-deep in motherhood but have a parent with mental health needs. Or you may have a new empty nest, but your husband has a debilitating condition. Or you're single in a job caring for others and you don't have someone to care for you at the end of a hard day.

Each situation requires gentle stewardship. But most of all, knowing you're not alone is important. God cares for you.

CULTIVATE STEWARDSHIP

I have used the word *calling* quite a bit in this chapter. While God calls us to steward others and nature, he also asks us to steward *that something* that is the soul seed of calling created inside you. Some people call it your talent, others your passion. Whatever it is, you need to steward it because the world needs it.

I believe that God ordains us to be in the time and space we are in, with all that he has created us to be. We are to nurture our greatest passions, asking God to show us how best to meet the needs of those he asks us to steward. He is inviting you to believe this too, so that others will see him through you.

Callings don't have to be elaborate. We each impact our circle of influence differently. Like my friend Cara, you may use your passion to benefit your family—she uses her training for occupational therapy to ensure her baby has developmentally stimulating surroundings. Or like Essie, you may infuse your calling into your professional life—she uses her interior design talent to create beautiful spaces for others.

You may steward your passion in other ways—weeding the garden, volunteering at a hospital, or crocheting afghans to give away. Whatever it is, it matters. If you're unsure, do the next thing for the person before you and see how God uses you to change the world.

SIMPLE SECRETS: NEXT STEPS

Now it's your turn. Here are simple suggestions to practice stewardship and uncomplicate your life:

- Identify your talent or passion, then give it away. Ideas may be:
  - Knit hats for a local school or blankets for a homeless shelter.
  - Paint a mug and give it to an older neighbor.
  - Use your humor to make someone laugh.
- Give financially or get involved with agencies that steward the environment, animals, or people.
- Babysit for a single mom in your church.
- Support local businesses of people of color.
- Become a trained CASA volunteer (Courted Appointed Special Advocates for children).

- Volunteer at a county or state park in your area.
- Visit and care for animals in a local animal shelter.
- Offer support services for families in your community who are foster parents.
- Pass out positive words of encouragement through texts or cards.
- Read a book on boundaries or restorative rest.

Prayer pause: *Invite Jesus to reveal what he desires for you from this chapter.*

REFLECTION

1. What time, talents, and treasures has God provided for you to steward in your current season?
2. Who in your life exemplifies stewardship? How would you like to emulate them?
3. What did you learn from this chapter that is most helpful, or what reflects your needs and hopes? How can you apply it to your life?
4. What is one lesson of stewardship from your life that you can retell to another person?

Chapter 8

{INTERDEPENDENCE}

Blessed Be the Ties that Bind

Compassion is the keen awareness of the interdependence of all things.

—Thomas Merton[1]

I walked into the barn and called Stella, our milking goat, to her stanchion. Ron was gone, so milking our dairy goat was my job. It had already been a long day working with domestic violence and foster care cases. Standing amidst straw and dried manure was an odd place to be after one of the most challenging days as a mental health provider. But the barn felt like a refuge.

Stella stared at me and snorted, letting me know she would rather see Ron than me. I sassed back at her, grabbed her collar, and guided her up a few steps to the wooden platform where she stood for milking. I took my hand and wiped off her belly, then grabbed her teats and leaned into her side, milking her by hand. The swish-swish of the milk into the bucket was therapeutic for me.

My mind wandered to Stella's presence in my day. Typically milking her would be an irritating chore to check off my list. Today its familiarity was soothing. Seeing her milk rise in the bowl reminded me that while she depended on me to relieve her full udder, I depended on her for our family's milk.

The process had a larger meaning. God was showing me that his rhythms between nature and humanity are reciprocal. We need one another. We humans are not silos unto ourselves. While humans create complicated problems that sometimes seem unsolvable, things in nature still work. While I cared for others, Stella took care of me.

WHAT WE NEED

Nature has an incredible way of reminding us that we are not self-reliant. On one of the first days of the lockdown in 2020, I watched the birds fly to and from our bird feeders. I was anxious and worried, but the birds weren't. I remembered what Jesus said in Matthew 6: God amply provides for each bird; would he not care for us even more? With each trip back and forth between the trees and the feeders, God showed me the interdependent relationship between him, me, and nature. God would also provide for my daily needs as he does for each animal.

The pandemic revealed how intricately we depend on one another in all aspects of life. The horses and buggies that clip-clopped by our home reminded me that nature's processes still worked, no matter how far humanity or technology evolves. Others learned this too, as many turned to nature during the pandemic. RV travel increased; people went to parks and rode bikes. Perhaps, like me, you sought and found God in new ways during that time, reminding us of how interconnected and interdependent we are.

INTERDEPENDENCE: THE EIGHTH SECRET

Interdependence—the eighth secret for a compelling life—is a vulnerable yet beautiful reliance and dependence upon someone or something outside ourselves. It is mutual reciprocity of support, intimacy, and trust where two or more entities rely on each other to help fulfill needs, whether they are physical, emotional, social, or spiritual. God intends interdependence for the church, families, community, nature, and the Godhead.

Genesis reveals a mesmerizing pattern of separating and joining with every living being. God separated the light from darkness and joined waters to create land. He created humans for mutual companionship with each other, him, and nature. God set all of them—beasts, himself, and humans—to coexist in the garden of Eden, in relationship with each other.

You still see glimpses of reciprocal relationships in most small towns, rural neighborhoods, church bodies, and the neighborhood bar where everybody knows your name. My neighbor who provides driving services for the Amish remarked how several Amish families he drives helped with outdoor chores and household repairs after he had surgery. They didn't do it because they had to or because they owed him something, but because he had become part of their community. Interdependence is not a transactional relationship.

CITIZENSHIP IS NOT A BAD WORD

Community citizenship was one of the core values at an elementary school where I worked. Though citizenship is a buzzword that may conjure controversial topics for some, it is not a bad word. At the school, we explained citizenship to students as being members of a community outside of ourselves that is interdependent upon one another. We see a need and help. We recycle and pick up trash in the hallway. We do what's best for the whole class while learning and growing as individuals. Separate, yet together.

Social media and instant communication have robbed students and many of us of mutual responsibility with and for others. We say things through a text or online comment that we would not say face-to-face, disregarding how words or actions affect others. This is antithetical to the nature of relationships God created.

Interdependence differs from stewardship because it's not exclusively caring for others—it is a mutual reliance upon others also caring for us. Psalm 68:6 says God puts the lonely in families. While God created families as the primary social relationship, the story of Israel in the Old Testament models how we are not just to care for our small nuclear family. We are called and responsible to give and receive mutual care, even as social systems and family structures change.

Dorie says she would not have been able to care for her husband when he needed constant caregiving if her family, church friends, community, and coworkers had not assisted her. Small things made a difference, like a coworker noticing if she was quieter than usual and others helping in the little areas of need.

THE BODY KNOWS

God created our minds, hearts, and bodies to interact with people and our environment. Our bodies release oxytocin, the bonding hormone, when our physical and emotional needs are met. A coworker meeting your needs and a parent responding to a baby's cry builds trust and attachment. Our bodies similarly respond to nature for health and safety needs.

For instance, we are naturally drawn to water and trees for sustenance and shelter, like those shade trees in Grandpa's yard. When listening to our body's red flags of danger, we instinctively avoid unsafe people or environments. And we respond with care when there is a need. As stewards of the land and one another, God uses the body of Christ to be his hands and feet.

When Ron's mom unexpectedly died, our community showed up. Amish and English neighbors and community members came to the farmhouse's back door, offering help to milk cows and do chores. The outpouring of care from others after her death was one of the many times I've seen God reveal himself through the community. It reminded me that we are not to do life alone.

I have seen more than one farm in our area whose owner died unexpectedly during harvest, only to have area farmers bring their combines, tractors, and semis to help harvest the crops. Though community interdependence is the cornerstone of Amish and Mennonite faith cultures, these practices aren't unique to Shipshewana—they can happen anywhere. It just takes one person to see a need and invite others to help.

We in the body of Christ are created for one another. Proverbs 27:17 says we care for and sharpen one another, giving and receiving care. In Acts 1:8, we read that we are to go out among our local neighborhoods, towns, and cities, sharing the gospel of Jesus Christ and being his presence on earth. We're not made to be holed up in an upper room with only a computer screen.

NATURE'S PLAYLAND

One year when I worked in a city school, I brought a small classroom of third- through sixth-grade students to the farm for a field trip. The kids had significant behavioral issues that impacted their success. All came from homes with adverse childhood experiences, such as a parent in jail, an addicted parent, or a home with family violence.

It was the first time the students had been on a farm. Several kids remarked they had never seen a cow or landscapes of large, open fields. Many didn't know that cows provided meat and milk they bought at stores. "This is amazing," was mumbled more than once as the students hand-fed goats in the goat pen or let kittens crawl on them in the grass.

The kids experienced what author Richard Louv calls *nature deficit disorder* in his book *The Last Child in the Woods*.[2] He describes it as a condition in which children lack unstructured interaction with nature, which results in minimized use of senses, problems with attention, propensity for obesity, and increased emotional and physical illness. Louv coined the term over twenty years ago, back when Millennials were being raised with organized sports, video games, and structured play. Since then, the internet arrived. Even in areas where kids can play outside, they spend more time inside than ever.

I have seen the adverse effects of this in my work. I was surprised one Monday morning when an agitated, crying kindergartener stated he didn't want to be at school. When I asked why, it wasn't because he missed his mom or feared something at school. He said he wanted to continue playing VR (virtual reality) because he'd been playing it all weekend. He was unable to transition from an unstructured, hours-long digitally stimulating experience of *virtual* reality to the less stimulating, *real-world* experience of going to school.

Kids don't need three-dimensional virtual experiences; they need the real deal of experiencing life that's all around them. Studies have proven that mental health is tied to nature interaction. And yet the average American child spends four to seven minutes daily in unstructured outdoor play versus seven hours on a screen.[3] Children growing up with the lowest levels of green space had up to 55 percent higher rates of developing psychiatric disorders.[4]

No matter where you live, making nature a playland doesn't take much. As a child, my mother-in-law made dolls from hollyhocks. My Italian grandparents' urban grapevine arbor was a mansion in my childhood imagination. Our kids squished cow manure between their toes or played whiffle ball for hours in our backyard. In nature kids learn confidence, imagination, and creativity—and adults can also reconnect with these essential skills.

Nature is important for us all. Take your kids for a ten-minute walk in your neighborhood or to a local park. Notice the trees, clouds, and insects. Eat your lunch outdoors while at work. Go on an outdoor scavenger hunt or visit your local botanical garden. Ride your bike or read a book on your apartment balcony. Whatever it takes, get outside.

THE ART OF RESPONSIBILITY

The *Memories of Hoosier Homemakers* series features an interview with a woman named Opal, who shared about cultural changes from her childhood. She remarked that kids have too much leisure time and little to do. "Children are better off having more responsibilities," she said.[5] That was forty years ago.

Today's generation has become even less healthy, more stressed, and more isolated due to the pressures and overuse of social media. Because they don't often have to get out from behind their screens, children don't know the interdependent social and work structures our forefathers did. They spend less time developing responsibility to the environment around them.

When Ron was six, it was his job to feed the cows when they came in to be milked. He learned young that crops, animals, and others relied on his responsibility and work ethic. Similar expectations are still appropriate for children. Kids at young ages can learn to unload a dishwasher, put their laundry away, and help clean—not as a fun activity but as part of the family system where everyone is reliant on each other.

There is no question that it's easier to take a path of comfort, especially in parenting. Kids whine about doing chores, so you don't ask them to. Videos entertain them effortlessly for hours. But the more we make things comfortable, the more disconnected our kids are from natural learning processes and their responsibilities to their social and physical environments. The same is true for us. We need to get out and engage with those around us.

I SEE YOU

One day, when I was teaching at our local high school, I stayed home with my sick toddler. The following day, a student said, "Mrs. Yoder, you played hooky. I saw you with your kid yesterday, sitting in your house." Our screen door was open when Nyla's bus passed our house. She saw right in.

That's not the first time I realized everyone knows your business in a small town. It's the downside of living in and among your community. But you also have an opportunity for belonging, reciprocity, and responsibility when you see, interact, and connect with neighbors and those in your sphere of influence. This is not exclusive to small rural areas.

My sisters have always lived in cities, and they build community by hosting gatherings, attending sporting events, and caring for their neighbors. You can build connections wherever you are: in the workplace, the gym, Bible study, or the drive-through. I try to smile and make eye contact with cashiers and sales clerks, perhaps saying hello or asking about their day. Just a tiny interaction lets them know they are seen.

INTERDEPENDENCE OVERLOAD

We can't discuss interdependence without mentioning enmeshment and codependency. Enmeshment is when a person is overly reliant and dependent upon someone or something else and no longer functions with autonomy and independence. Codependency is an unhealthy relationship where two people rely too much on each other and lose their own sense of self, often letting the problems of one overtake the life of the other. In contrast, interdependence requires people to operate independently and help one another thrive.

People in codependent relationships have a false sense of helping someone in need, such as an addict or loved one. One becomes the rescuer in the name of love or cares in a way that prevents the person being rescued from being responsible or accountable for their actions, choices, or outcomes. The rescuer's life is consumed with the problems of the one they love. Lack of autonomy prevents either person from taking responsibility for healthy change.

Similar patterns can appear in other relationships, such as friendships, romantic relationships, marriages, and families. Failing to release children at appropriate developmental stages also enables codependence and enmeshment, especially in young adulthood. (My book *Fledge: Launching Your Kids Without Losing Your Mind* is a great resource). Having children with addictions or mental health needs makes it more difficult to distinguish the fine line between healthy support and codependence. Professional help is best when you're unsure how to navigate these tensions and when firm boundaries are needed,

THIS IS THE BODY OF CHRIST

When Ron had his logging accident, we didn't know how long his recovery would be or how many weeks or months he would be off work. We had impending hospital bills. Then our car died on the way home from the hospital and needed significant repairs.

After becoming aware of our immediate financial needs, a friend asked if she could set up an account where friends and family could help offset our medical expenses and lack of income during his recovery. It felt vulnerable to be in a position where we needed help, and I hesitated to accept her offer. Then she reminded me that helping one another is what Christians do.

Love gives but also receives. We were humbled by the generosity of others who responded. The experience taught me how beautiful, delicate, and vulnerable interdependence is. God didn't intend for us to experience life without support and reciprocity. We need one another in times of need, and others need us.

Genesis 28:14 says all people will be blessed through *you*. People need you in their life. I often feel like I don't do enough for others or God. Perhaps you feel this way, too.

God showed me something recently when reading Hebrews 6:10. The verse says God will not forget your work and the love you show him *as you have helped his people*. Through this God showed me that he receives our acts of helping others as a gesture of love and worship. Serving another isn't a works-based checklist. It's another example of the reciprocal relationship between us, God, and each other.

Some days now, when I drive home from a challenging workday, I praise God for the opportunity to worship him through my work helping others. The perspective uncomplicates my faith life. I am comforted that I don't have to do more to show God my love. I feel deep satisfaction knowing there is sacred space between us humans, each other, and God.

The same is true for you. Each act of kindness you show someone in your home, workplace, or going about your day is an act of love and worship toward God. Listening to a coworker's troubles, making a meal for a friend, or other acts of kindness are active demonstrations of your love for God that can uncomplicate your faith life too.

A NEW MINDSET

I recently texted a coworker about a project we were working on. I needed her to complete her portion before I could do my assigned steps. At the end of the text, I said, "Thank you." She replied, "You're welcome." Those two words caused an internal reaction I was unprepared for.

It was humbling to receive the words "You're welcome." Usually, we hear "No worries" or "No problem," which minimizes our ask. Receiving "You're welcome" acknowledges we had a need the other person met. The two words exposed my own sense of pride and self-sufficiency.

It's challenging to accept words of "You're welcome" because it is even more challenging to ask for help. Our son and daughter-in-law teach our toddler grandsons to say "Help" rather than whine when frustrated or in need. It's a mindset we adults need to practice. Our culture of self-reliance teaches us to do things ourselves. We get angry or give up when we can't. Like a child, we need to learn to ask for help.

I recently encountered a distressed woman walking alongside the road carrying a loose bundle of clothes. Having worked in domestic violence, I am sensitive to such situations. I stopped and asked if she needed help. Based on her needs, I was able to get her connected with resources. She was embarrassed to be in a situation where she needed help. I understood that. I simply told her to pay it forward when she could. She smiled, saying yes, she would pay it forward.

Interdependence informs a mindset that God created us for one another. We can give and receive freely. When you can't repay an act of service, return the favor to someone else when you can. Do for others as someone has done for you.

Romans 12:13 says, "Share with the Lord's people who are in need." You may feel uncomfortable helping a stranger by the road or at your door. No worries. Wherever God places you in your circle of influence, learn the new mindset and language of "Help" and "You're welcome."

SCRIPTURE APPLICATION

Every page of the Bible tells stories of interdependence, with the pinnacle being the gospel itself. God gave his son, Jesus Christ, to walk among us. Jesus gave his life for us so we can restore our relationship with God, one another, and creation. Upon salvation, we receive the Holy Spirit. John 15 says Jesus is the vine, and we are the branches. Apart from him, we can do nothing.

Scripture also reminds us of our responsibility to one another. Romans 14:7 says "none of us lives for ourselves alone, and none of us dies for ourselves alone." Dorie told me that when others wanted to help her when her husband was sick, it was difficult to accept; she wanted to do most things herself. But she eventually realized she couldn't do everything. Though it was hard, she learned to reach out to friends, family, and her church community.

Further, Romans 14:19 says we are to make every effort to do what leads to peace and mutual edification. We give and receive counsel from one another. We help each other. We listen with empathy. We are vulnerable with our hurts. Now that Dorie is a widow, she gives back to others in little areas when she can—taking a coffee to an older widow, helping with a young mom, and using her journey to assist others.

AN INTERDEPENDENCE LIFESTYLE

How do you make interdependence a lifestyle? It doesn't have to be through Amish barn raisings, which are often romanticized. Typical acts are much smaller happenings. While writing this book, two young moms I mentor surprised me by bringing a few meals and snacks to get me through the long days of writing and editing. It was a beautiful gesture of reciprocity.

The same day I received their meals, I attended the wedding of a friend who had experienced ongoing grief and hardship. Several friends were there celebrating with her, each of us having a unique role in her journey. We watched as God began restoring the years the locusts had eaten (Joel 2:25).

1 Corinthians 12 describes the unity and diversity of the body of Christ. One part doesn't function without the other. Verses 25 and 26 say there should be no division in the body but that its features should have equal concern for each other. If one part suffers, every part suffers; if one part is honored, every part rejoices.

Serving the body of Christ through your spiritual gifts, time, and talents is one of the most rewarding ways to practice reciprocity. But reciprocity by nature is a two-way relationship. With your church roles, build in periods of sabbath rest where you aren't actively volunteering so you can get replenished. Self-reliance says, "If I don't do it, no one else will." Interdependence says a person with a gift is waiting to take their part of the body of Christ while you step away and rest.

LET GO OF SELF-RELIANCE

What is holding you back from growing in interdependence? Like me, you may need to let go of self-reliance. You may have been raised that you don't ask for help or been taught that there's always someone worse off than yourself. Growing in interdependence may mean having awkward conversations of vulnerability by asking for help or accepting "You're welcome." God invites us to receive his care through the support or presence of others.

We also may need to let go of stubbornness in thinking we don't need to ask God for our needs. We've discussed Philippians 4:6–7 before, but it's worth revisiting. In this passage, God asks us to present our needs and requests to him. In reciprocity, he promises to give us his peace that transcends all understanding to guard our hearts and minds in Christ Jesus. Interdependence is a posture of hands open to receive from God the riches he desires to pour out.

Finally, let go of devices and get outside! God provides the sun, moon, and stars in all locations on the earth. Explore your community's nature and find what you enjoy. Since the pandemic, Ron and I have discovered we enjoy getting away outdoors and camping in a small travel trailer.

CULTIVATE INTERDEPENDENCE

Sarah and Amelia are two writer friends who are also my prayer partners. We live in different cities and share weekly prayer requests through text or a video app. We started these weekly prayers years ago to bridge the isolation writers often feel. At first we shared professional needs. Then came more personal requests—parenting struggles, doubts, and discouragement. Mutual vulnerability and encouragement took shape. This interdependent relationship is now an essential rhythm in my life.

Similarly, there are rhythms in nature and the world where interdependence makes a difference to all parties. We care for nature and the animals on the farm, and they return such care. Clean bedding and quality feed for cows ensures milk in our cups. In the marketplace, fair trade goods provide food on another's table. No matter where we live, we witness and participate in interdependence, even as God draws us to himself and invites us to respond.

Love gives, and love receives.

SIMPLE SECRETS: NEXT STEPS

Now it's your turn. Here are simple suggestions to practice interdependence and uncomplicate your life:

- Invite a coworker out for coffee or invite a neighbor for a walk.
- Allow your adult kids to help you if they offer; have your younger kids help with family chores.
- Plan in-person meet-ups or gatherings with online friends.
- Practice saying, "You're welcome," and "I need help." Pay something forward.
- Take neighborhood walks, visit local parks, or sit in your backyard or apartment balcony without your phone. Listen to the sounds.
- Plant something new in your yard or patio container. Try indoor plants or get a bird feeder.
- Volunteer at the local animal shelter or walk a neighbor's dog.
- Involve your kids and grandchildren in recycling or safely pick up trash in your neighborhood or local park.
- Purchase sustainable products. Shop at your local farmer's market or support local farm-to-table restaurants.

- Incorporate nature into spiritual practices. Read the Bible outside. Go to a park to reflect and pray.
- Practice gratitude for nature around you—the sunrise, blue skies, rain, and snow.

Prayer pause: *Invite Jesus to reveal what he desires for you from this chapter.*

REFLECTION

1. How do you struggle with self-reliance and independence rather than interdependence?
2. Who is one person in your life who models interdependence? What do you learn from them, or what would you like to emulate?
3. What did you learn from this chapter that is most helpful, or what reflects your needs and hopes? How can you apply it to your life?
4. What is one lesson of interdependence from your life that you can retell to another person?

Chapter 9

{GROUNDEDNESS AND HUMILITY}

Authentic and Real

Farming must be approached with great humility. The learned man, the really learned one, is aware that he knows very little.

—Catherine Doherty[1]

I was traveling home from a speaking event in a prestigious suburban community, very content with how it went. Several women thanked me for my counseling and parenting advice, making me feel valued, respected, and appreciated as a professional. I drove home on the freeway, jamming to music in the sunshine that reflected my upbeat and confident mood.

When I pulled into my driveway, I mentally transitioned to the parenting duties awaiting me: dinner to make, laundry to do, and groceries for my teen athletes. As I switched roles from esteemed speaker to mundane mom, I opened the kitchen door and stood stock still.

On my dining room table was a dead, stuffed squirrel sitting on a log, looking right at me.

"I should expect nothing less," I muttered under my breath. One moment, you're a well-respected expert speaking to many; the next, you're moving a dead squirrel off your table so your family can eat.

There's no chance for ego on a farm. You're wearing high heels one moment and chasing a cow off the road the next. If you're lucky, you have time to change shoes. Humility grows right alongside the corn here on the farm. Most rural folks are not far from a manure pile or an animal that won't put up with them. Creation is your classroom; folk knowledge is your degree. Tomorrow is another day that can make or break you.

THE LESS-THAN-PERFECT LIFE

These principles are true for all of us, no matter where we live. Life is messy and unpredictable, yet we cling to the picture-perfect image. Author Jill Savage says we compare our insides to other people's outsides. Her *No More Perfect* books on marriage, motherhood, and parenting are great resources to dispel the idealization of family life.[2] We all are one open door away from a stuffed squirrel, a rebellious teen, or a spouse who walks out.

Such resources weren't available to me when I was a struggling wife and mom. I tried my best, but I often crawled into bed at night feeling like a failure. I longed to read about or see someone who wasn't the Proverbs 31 superwoman. I needed an authentic, honest, and approachable person who would listen to my struggles in my less-than-perfect life, whose feet were in life's dirt and mud, and who would stand there with me. I wanted to hear that while things were hard, God was still present. That somehow, things would be okay.

I wondered if anyone else was out there whose life didn't meet the storybook image. I started my blog, *Life Beyond the Picket Fence,* during this time. I used that analogy because our white picket fence borders our garden. Beyond it are weeds, dirt, and manure. But it's amidst those smelly and messy things that good things still grow.

GROUNDED AND HUMBLE: THE NINTH SECRET

Being grounded and humble—the ninth secret—is what farm life gives you. A grounded person has *that something* you recognize when you encounter them. One may describe it as being sensible and down-to-earth. Another visual metaphor is of having your feet on the ground, which means you are firmly connected to reality; your head is not in the clouds. A grounded person is authentic and genuine.

By formal definition, a grounded person is mentally and emotionally stable, realistic, and unpretentious. They value ordinary things in life and have a sense of who they are, where they came from, and where they are going. Not much uproots their values and convictions, even when life is hard. They have clarity about why they do what they do.

Rural life is grounding. There is history and familiarity with your surroundings. Many rural people live near family. The corn that's knee-high by the Fourth of July is the same landscape as when you were young. Coming home means returning to a house and the dirt that holds your ancestors' blood, sweat, and tears. That's the feeling I had at Grandpa's farm; perhaps you know the same feeling, too.

Grounding is also a universal human experience. Farmers, naturalists, and hikers instinctively know that touching land and being in nature helps emotional, mental, and physical health. *Grounding* and *mindfulness* are more clinical and spiritual terms for similar experiences that center your thoughts and senses in your environment. Deep breathing, listening to sounds around you, and touching the textures near you—all help bring momentary peace and relaxation.

My friend Elizabeth has recently learned the benefit of such experiences. Though out of shape most of her life, she started hiking to get in shape for a camping trip to the bottom of the Grand Canyon and hasn't stopped. She did not anticipate the physical, mental, and emotional benefits that hiking and sleeping outside would have on her life.

HUMBLE POSTURES

Being close to nature also humbles you. It's difficult to boast when you're shoveling cow manure or standing in the presence of a stenchy billy goat. But location or lifestyle doesn't make one humble. Even in the concrete jungle, picking up after your dog reminds you that everyone handles some crap.

Humility doesn't come naturally to us as humans. Historically, Amish and Mennonite faith traditions include the posture of footwashing as a faith practice of humility and serving one another, reminding participants of the interdependent relationship of community. It's a practice modeled after Jesus washing the disciples' feet in John 13. Our congregation still practices footwashing twice yearly during communion services.

It's a vulnerable and humble status to take off your shoes, kneel before a water basin, and wash another person's feet. Seeing and touching someone's cal_louses, rinsing their skin, and patting tender parts of their body is an intimate experience. It's even more sobering to have the same done for you.

AUTHENTIC LEADERS

Humility is not something we see daily. When we do, it stands out. My sons had their first jobs as young teens doing dirty, menial outdoor work for a local business. One of the owners worked alongside the kids and gently mentored them on how to do a thorough job. The businessman's humble demeanor and gentle spirit—especially as a community leader—was a poignant example of authentic servant leadership.

Grounded, humble people get their hands dirty in life's matters, no matter their station in life. They are the same no matter where they go. That squirrel on the table reminded me that while others may esteem me professionally, I'm just an ordinary mom whose hands touch the dirty things in life, along with my kid whose hands stuffed a dead rodent in agriculture class. Such things keep your pride in check.

One day at school, I was helping a student in the hallway who had twisted a comb in her long hair that she could not get out. I made several attempts to untangle the mess. The principal walked past us, assessed the situation, and said, "Let me help you with that." Wearing a skirt and heels, she put her papers down and carefully worked with the tangled mess until the comb was out.

When I grow up, I want to be a leader like that.

These are people—and there are many of them—whose meaningful acts are obscure to most. Often integrity is measured by what one does or does not do in private—spoonfeeding a debilitated spouse, not bowing to intimidation, or not compromising values. Humble people don't view what they do as anything special. It's just part of their life and who they are.

You, too, have moments like these, and you may overlook them. But God doesn't. Psalm 84:11 says God does not withhold good things from those whose walk is upright. Humility helps us resist the temptation to share these moments on social media as our culture tells us to post everything we do for affirmation and acceptance. But there is no need because God sees every act of goodness you do when no one else does. Those precious and private moments are sacred.

IN THE BACK ROW

I was on staff at a writer's conference where most attendees were women. During a break, we were instructed to introduce ourselves to someone we had not met yet. I scanned my area for some first-time attendees who might feel nervous being among more experienced writers.

Sitting in the back of the room, I noticed an older gentleman at a table by himself. No one had greeted him yet. I approached him with a smile, shook his hand, and welcomed him to the conference. I gave myself an A-plus for hospitality.

That evening, our keynote speaker took the stage. It was none other than the humble individual I thought I was welcoming as a beginning writer. He has written over one hundred books and publications.

Humble people don't tell you who they are. They just *are*.

People marked by humility and authenticity don't tout privileges or power, whether intelligence, accomplishments, wealth, or influence. They have a posture of being among others that doesn't draw attention to themselves. I have a friend who is from a family of significant influence and wealth, but I had known her for several months before I knew this. She lives modestly and works in a people-helping profession serving the most vulnerable. She leads a compelling life not because of her status or money, but because of her humility and authenticity.

YOU CAN'T FOOL THEM

There's a saying that people don't care how much you know until they know how much you care. This is especially true for teens. They are the most skeptical people you will meet. They sniff out pride and hypocrisy like nobody's business. I was baptized in authenticity by working with teens as a parent and teacher.

As a young mom of teens, I learned humility and authenticity when saying sorry as the first step in a relationship repair, rather than clinging to my pride by not admitting I was wrong. I wish I had learned this earlier, though. For years I carried guilt and grief for things I wish I could have done differently. Perhaps you have, too. Instead of self-condemnation or arrogant denial, humility allows us to accept that we did the best we knew at the time. When we know differently, we do better.

Similarly, one of the first pieces of advice given to me as a beginning teacher to high schoolers was not to pretend that I knew something if I did not. Instead, I should tell students I would find the answer and get back to them. This felt vulnerable as it did when I apologized to my children. But it's sound wisdom. Kids won't tell you, but they value honesty and authenticity more than a prideful adult who strives to prove they are right. Authentic, grounded adults make kids feel secure, especially in a culture of instability.

UNTETHERED AND BLOWING IN THE WIND

Today's teens have few such role models. In a May 2023 interview on *Face the Nation*, former Defense Secretary Robert Gates cited meanness and lack of civility among politicians as the greatest threat to our nation.[3] I'd agree, adding leaders in all other spheres to this list. In addition, research on kindness and empathy has shown that both attributes have declined in recent years, coinciding with a rise in narcissism.[4]

This cultural unraveling is affecting our youth. Rising anxiety and depression among teens and young adults mirror the chaos around them. They need adults who make them feel safe, secure, and at home with themselves. Kids are grounded when their needs for belonging and safety are met. Otherwise they live in an untethered state of perpetually trying to find ways to meet those needs, often looking to unhealthy people or unsafe experiences.

James 1:5–6 gives a good picture of being untethered: it's like being a leaf in the wind, vulnerable and easily swayed. "If any of you lacks wisdom, you should ask God, who gives generously to all without finding fault, and it will be given to you. But when you ask, you must believe and not doubt, because the one who doubts is like a wave of the sea, blown and tossed by the wind."

I wonder if many of us feel tossed and blown around with doubt and uncertainty. The fast-paced, ever-changing, information-driven culture saturates us without ever satisfying us. These things feel disingenuous, even if our own life is not. I long for the wisdom described in James rather than the latest memes from Instagram influencers. I want sound truth that grounds my mind, values, and choices.

A NEW MINDSET

For several years before the pandemic, I was a full-time speaker, writer, and therapist working from home. It sounds great, but it was often isolating and lonely as I traveled and was online a lot. My kids were in college or on their own. I no longer attended school events, where I had socialized for over twenty years. I felt untethered and disconnected from my previous in-person life.

I spent much time planning for things outside of my physical environment—social media posts, promotional videos, etc. I wanted social media–free days and longed for a hands-on life where I engaged in work and relationships I could touch and feel. I wanted to do things like weed my flower beds and mentor a few local women rather than be online. I wanted to be more present in my life. I had to develop a mindset to embrace and live out those values.

The pandemic permitted me to reclaim a lifestyle that matched my heart. When all things went virtual, I disembarked. I declined most online speaking events. Rather than conduct long-term virtual therapy, I accepted a part-time school counseling position. Developing in-person relationships with students and peers was life-changing. It grounded me when so much else changed. For this season, here is where I am most at home with myself and connected with what is most important to me.

Perhaps you too are searching for the people, places, or experiences that make you feel grounded and at home. Many of us are still searching for the stability we lost at the start of the pandemic. That's one reason for this book. Visitors flock to our area because the rural Amish lifestyle reminds them of *that something* or someone that will ground them, returning them to what they know.

All of us can acquire the grounded life we long for. Each season is a different journey with unique needs and new opportunities to reassess priorities. We will feel uprooted and untethered when our minds, hearts, hands, and feet run in different directions. It is finding what brings them back home that grounds our souls.

MILKHOUSE MENTORING

Some of the things that ground me are old things, processes, and people. I'm most at home in antique stores, museums, back roads, and among stories of bygone eras. These relics stand the test of time, telling me things will be okay. Their stories of survival invite me to lower my roots into today's soil and shelter someone else, as others have done for me.

In the first decade of our marriage, some of the most grounding moments happened in the dimly lit old milkhouse and barn. Each fall, the milking cows gave birth to dozens of calves. In the early morning, while the men milked, my sisters-in-law, mother-in-law, and I took turns bottle-feeding calves. There I learned much about life.

I was taught to be gentle yet firm, straddling a newborn calf to help it drink. You had to let it suck on your fingers until its tongue knew what to do. The bottle you fed it had to be at the right angle for the calf's health and safety. I watched, and then I did.

I learned other things, too. We discussed family happenings, worries, and hopes while washing milk bottles and rinsing the cement floor with hot, steamy water. I received a foundation for womanhood that couldn't be scripted or preplanned. Such interactions were how people have mentored and learned from each other throughout time.

I still crave these experiences. Ron and I taught our church's eighty- and ninety-year-olds' Sunday school class right before the pandemic. These were the faith giants I have watched for decades. We were supposed to teach them, but I was happy to sit among these elders and glean their wisdom.

These kinds of experiences are like entering a stable home. You want to stay and never leave. But life changes. My life has changed, as has yours. We can't live in the past. God calls us not to look back and remain. Instead, we should bring that stability with us. No matter where we dwell, we can grow deep roots and then shade others with the influence that has been given to us.

SCRIPTURE APPLICATION

There's a saying that the older you get, the less you know. I think that's true. One of the most senior women in our church used to say that she didn't know much, but she'd tell you what God taught her that morning. She was one of those heroes I want to emulate. Her life was sometimes challenging, but she was a student of it.

Life often has situations for which there are no answers. Recognizing this is the place of true humility. "Lean not on your own understanding," says Proverbs 3:5. When the bottom of life falls out, you can have assurance that God's word and character will hold you up.

Jeremiah 17:7–8 says, "Blessed is the one who trusts in the LORD, whose confidence is in him. They will be like a tree planted by the water that sends out its roots by the stream. It does not fear when heat comes; its leaves are always green. It has no worries in a year of drought and never fails to bear fruit."

I want these roots, like the older people whose shade I've stood under. I imagine you do too. So do our families, youth, and communities. We need deep roots, strong branches, sheltering shade, and beautiful fruit. We need grounding, humble people tethering the soil that, without them, erodes with each storm.

MAKE GROUNDEDNESS AND HUMILITY A LIFESTYLE

Living in the same small community where you teach presents challenges. You can't be one person in the classroom and then another in real life. People know your character, good or bad. They know where you live. It provides accountability.

In one of the first years I taught, a teen shared some hard things about their home life with me. They reached a point in the conversation when they pulled back in the chair and hesitated.

I looked into their eyes and considered the context of what they were sharing. Their mom was single and worked two jobs.

Our home, with its well-manicured lawn and white picket fence garden, was very different from theirs. During a pause, I said, "You think I live in a fairy tale world, don't you?"

Their "Yes" taught me a significant lesson in life's curriculum that I'm still learning.

My life and how I see things is only one perspective of the billions on earth. There are moments in the counseling office, at speaking events, or talking with a parent when I realize God has allowed me to be in a sacred space in someone's life. You have those moments, too. It's holy ground there, worthy of taking off your sandals and standing in awe of God bearing his image in another human, so different yet alike.

This is where humanity considers who we are in relationship to Jesus. We are made from the ground, and to the ground we will return. Only through Christ in us, connecting with God's image in another, do we feel the earth beneath us and realize that the ground is level at the foot of the cross.

As a therapist, I've learned that everyone is the expert in their own stories. Therefore we must be teachable, curious about one another, and not arrogant. Your life experiences, authenticity, and vulnerability give sacred space for someone else to be seen and known.

LET GO OF PRIDE AND INSECURITY

Growing up, Ron was taught fearful reverence and humility toward the bulls in the cow herd. When he brought the female cows in for the morning milking, Ron had to approach the bull humbly but confidently, recognizing and respecting each of their roles, knowing the bull could sense any insecurities and destroy him.

It's a powerful image of grounded humility and respect for ourselves and others. Ron had to relinquish any pride or insecurity to do his job safely. He had to respect his role humbly and that of the bull to do his job. Likewise, it's wise of us to let go of pride and insecurity, realizing our limitations to do the work God asks of us. This is where authentic humility grows.

Letting go of pride and insecurity is also frightening. They act as defense mechanisms to shield us from what is underneath them. Without them, we are left to contend with our true selves, both our strengths and our weaknesses. An authentic, grounded person does not need pride or insecurity because she is comfortable in her own skin.

That is what I needed so much of my life. I looked to places, people, or experiences to feel accepted. I needed to let go of the pride I received in being the perfect wife and mom. I needed to let go of the insecurities and shame that made me feel like everything about me was wrong. Perhaps you need to let go of these things, too.

We don't need to be afraid when we let go of these protective shields. What is left behind is the remarkable creature God created us to be, with limitations but also beauty. It's God's invitation to come home to an authentic, uncomplicated life where both our humanity and Jesus reside. Humility breeds confidence in how God created us while also acknowledging our need for him.

CULTIVATE AUTHENTICITY AND HUMILITY

I never realized my need for God more than when he was working with me to change my reactive behaviors as a parent. When I overreacted or said hurtful words, I had to let go of pride and attempt to repair the relationship. One day, I wrote a note asking one of my children for forgiveness rather than apologizing with empty words. I started with, "I'm sorry for my hurtful words. But when you. . . ."

The Holy Spirit stopped me. After three attempts to blame my teen, God impressed upon me that I must be entirely responsible for what I said without any blame or justification. It was a vulnerable moment, one where I felt true humility. I realized my depravity and the need for God to work in my life; on my own, I had failed.

When I received my child's forgiveness that day, it was the first time I truly felt grace—undeserved kindness of which I was not worthy. Then I realized the fullness of God's forgiveness and grace we receive because of Christ's payment for our sins on the cross. That moment was also the beginning of my journey home—that place where being honest with yourself and God is the foundation of authenticity. God digs up the pride in our lives and roots out the weeds drowning the fruit of the Holy Spirit. Accepting our limitations opens a river of life, grace, and freedom.

This is what it means to live an authentic, uncomplicated life. You keep what is most needed and lose the rest. There's not much here but a limited understanding of life's futility, humanity's frailty, and God's faithfulness. It's not exclusive to the Amish, our grandmothers, or farmers. It goes with you wherever you go, tethering itself to the beautiful life God has given you, bearing fruit for generations to come.

SIMPLE SECRETS: NEXT STEPS

Now it's your turn. Here are simple suggestions to practice groundedness and humility and uncomplicate your life:

- Practice listening to others with curiosity about their story and history.
- Laugh at humorous or embarrassing situations you find yourself in.

- Intentionally interact with someone unlike yourself.
- Spend more time doing something with your hands—write, sew, make jewelry, build a table.
- Ask an older adult about their life. Mentor someone in your circle.
- Walk outside barefoot on the grass or in a mud puddle after it rains.
- Learn about another culture different from your own.
- Think of people or places where you can be yourself. Cultivate more of these experiences.
- Practice grounding techniques like deep breathing or reflective journaling in the morning or evening to clear your mind and heart.
- Make a practice of asking for forgiveness.
- Practice footwashing with your spouse or children.

Prayer pause: *Invite Jesus to reveal what he desires for you from this chapter.*

REFLECTION

1. In what area of your life do you need to cultivate vulnerability, teachability, or letting go of pride?
2. Who is one person in your life who models authenticity or humility? What do you learn from them or what would you like to emulate?
3. What did you learn from this chapter that is most helpful, or what reflects your needs and hopes? How will you apply it to your life?
4. What is one lesson of grounding or humility from your life that you can retell to another person?

Chapter 10

An Heirloom Life

"Stand at the crossroads and look; ask for the ancient paths, ask where the good way is, and walk in it, and you will find rest for your souls."
—Jeremiah 6:16

When Ron's grandpa asked us to live on his heirloom-like farm after our engagement, I thought the dreams of my youth were coming true. Grandpa's farm had *that something* that met the longings I had searched for in so many other places. There was no pressure to be someone I wasn't on the simple homestead where little had changed and time seemed to stand still. Its wide-open spaces surrounded by older Amish farms didn't fence me in.

To me, it was like coming home.

I imagined our future kids running through the yard or playing house in the summer kitchen. The old farmhouse was just like the ones I dreamed of, with generations of stories waiting to inform another generation. The farm contained so many dreams I couldn't quite name—*that something* of a compelling, uncomplicated life.

Then Ron's grandma died a few months after we were invited to live there. Grandpa remained on his farm for two more decades living a legacy lifestyle that grounds you— raising cattle, growing a garden, using age-old farming practices. Grandpa was healthy and active until he died at one hundred in the same bedroom where he was born.

Grandpa had seen many changes in his life. The internet arrived before his death. And so had our complicated lives.

YOUR SOUL SEED

Grandpa's farm was the place where I seemed to physically touch *that something* I had searched for most of my life. A place of longing and belonging that God implants as a soul seed early in our lives—dreams we think should grow immediately. Instead, those seeds remain dormant, something we daydream about as life gets complicated. The kids come. The divorce happens. Loved ones die. We keep moving on, doing the next thing.

Sometimes the tension between that soul seed and life's reality makes you feel stuck. Many days you may wonder how pieces of your life fit together, especially when what you thought your life would be is not what you are living. I've spent so much of my life living in this tension as things changed over time. Maybe you have, too.

We never lived at Grandpa's. Instead, we built a house near Ron's family farm. I looked forward to being near his parents where I could give back to them in their old age as they had given to me. Then so many of life's good things changed. Ron's mom died, a loss that can't be described. The dairy cows were eventually sold, an ending both welcomed and mourned. Ron and I struggled with life's complications in ways that many young families do.

The summer of Grandpa's estate sale, more things were changing. I turned forty that year and left teaching to reclaim a less stressful life. I mourned that loss, too. My passion for history, teaching, and mentoring had converged in my US history classroom. *That something* was there. But it was time for a new *something* to take its place. I was starting full-time graduate school a few days after Grandpa's auction.

But on that sale day, so many life threads converged at once—grief, excitement, the soul seed I couldn't quite name. Standing in the shadow of Grandpa's farmhouse, I asked God why such a simple dream of living there didn't work out. He whispered back to my heart with a voice that perhaps you know. Jesus impressed upon me that while I perceived the best life was supposed to be there or with the people and experiences I mourned, he had something better.

Jesus invited me to consider that the compelling life I was created for wasn't in a place or with certain people. It's more of a journey between the past and the future to be lived in the present. He taught me those soul seeds he planted within me were foresight—*that something* that informs our dreams and guides our present so that we live with no regrets.

FORESIGHT: THE TENTH SECRET

Foresight—the tenth secret—is the final virtue that creates a compelling, uncomplicated life. Foresight is a type of wisdom that anticipates what may happen or will be needed in the future. Its counterparts are insight—the ability to understand a person or situation deeply, and hindsight—an understanding of a situation after it's occurred.

Foresight is *that something* that years ago packed a hope chest for a new bride. It included housekeeping items and heirloom things for future children. A tablecloth your grandmother made. A glass ornament that would start new traditions. You hoped each of these treasures would be passed down to yet another generation, with stories of your life passed down, too.

Foresight is also a companion to prudence. It strategically plans and applies knowledge and experience to things yet to come. It sees future needs while getting through challenges and current seasons. The Amish use foresight when considering how new technologies may impact their lifestyles. Farmers use it to predict what's needed for next year's crops.

Foresight people are heritage and legacy people—the people we want to be but struggle to be in our live-for-today generation. Heritage refers to a person's unique, inherited family identity: the values, traditions, culture, and artifacts passed down from previous generations. Legacy is the long-lasting impact of events, actions, or a person's life. These qualities are still embedded in many worldwide cultures, but we have mostly traded their importance for a feel-good-now culture in America.

Let's relearn how to use foresight to create an uncomplicated life that leaves a compelling heritage and legacy.

EMPTY PROMISES

One hot August afternoon when I was canning peaches, Ron's dad called. "Mom's not feeling well. She says she can't breathe. The ambulance is taking her to the hospital." Lois had outpatient knee surgery the day before.

Ron had just come home from milking cows. Despite not knowing what was wrong, prudence told us to make the thirty-minute drive to the hospital. Ron called my mom to stay with the children, ages eight to eight months, while I went to tell the older kids where we were going.

I went to their bedrooms and shared that grandma wasn't feeling well and we were going to the hospital. One of the kids asked if Grandma would be okay. I was about to reply that she would be fine, but something caused me to pause.

Experiences on the farm taught me and the kids that life wasn't predictable. There aren't always happy endings. What if this wasn't just a precautionary trip? What if she was having a stroke or something debilitating? Foresight made me wonder what legacy I'd leave on a child's faith if I gave an empty promise and life turned out differently.

I asked God for wisdom. I responded that I wasn't sure if Grandma would be okay, but I knew God was with her. The Holy Spirit guided me to pray with my child that God would be with Grandma and us and that his will would be done in the situation.

We reached the hospital and gathered with Ron's family. We were still unprepared when the chaplain told us Lois had died from a blood clot in her lung.

PROGRESSIVE LENSES

I did not, I could not, predict that death was imminent for Ron's mom. Foresight synthesizes life experiences in real time, projecting their future impacts. It's like having progressive lenses. You see near and far simultaneously and adjust your view accordingly.

1 Chronicles 12:32 speaks of the men of Issachar who *understood the times* and knew what Israel should do. I love this description of how moments fit both in present and future contexts. It's like reading the weather when you step outside in the morning; your senses inform your day's choices.

Parents use foresight routinely, saving for college or teaching their values. When one of our teens wanted to go on an international mission trip during Christmas, I selfishly wanted to say no. Then I looked at the opportunity through the lens of our values. I wanted each child to have a cross-cultural experience before graduating to plant the seed of service and give them an opportunity to learn from other cultures.

Though the timing was imperfect, foresight informed me I needed to align my long-term priorities with the ask. That trip greatly influenced that teen's calling and vocation. It taught me to listen to my values when my emotions say otherwise.

LIVING LEGACY

When my mother-in-law died, she was only sixty-six. I grieved the loss of her presence in my children's lives. To make meaning of our grief, I wondered how I could create a living legacy of her memory. Foresight prompted me to identify specific qualities I valued in her life that the children would miss and that I could create for them.

With the older grandchildren, Lois had fostered simple memory-making experiences. These included picnics, tea parties, and day trips. I decided I could do such things in her place and reminded myself to talk about her influence throughout my children's lives. I started taking the kids on special excursions each summer, spending a day with each child individually. When the kids were in junior high, I took each of them on a memorable road trip.

Lois had also kept memorable things of heritage from her parents and grandparents that she shared with the grandkids. Antiques were to be enjoyed, not simply displayed. This prompted me over the years to keep old toys our kids played with, which our grandkids now enjoy. These small traditions create a heritage of family culture. They don't have to cost much or take much time.

Are there memories you want to foster or experiences you want to revisit? Just take the next step to make it a reality.

My friend Melena lost both of her parents within one year. She does several things to keep traditions and memories of her mom alive with her young children. One is making her mom's handmade dinner rolls from an old church recipe on the same table her mother used. Another tradition involves playing games and shooting Silly String at each other on New Year's Eve, just like Melena did growing up.

Foresight helps us not waste our daily experiences but prompts us to be intentional about what we hope for the future. What traditions or intentional practices have you thought about starting but haven't taken the time to do so? Such memorable activities don't have to be elaborate. My "Lois" moments often included stopping to do something silly rather than saying I don't have time. Maybe you simply watch sports with your kids or play a mean game of Monopoly with your nieces and nephews. Whatever memories you're making, they are creating your heritage and legacy.

JUST ONE GENERATION AWAY

Foresight seems more palatable for cultures with little change, as often seen in the Amish community. They understand that future generations are impacted when we change our current lifestyles. We see the effects of this on family farms as our modern ways of life make small farms less sustainable than a generation or two ago. I also see this as I drive along the back roads of communities. Once-thriving towns that now have boarded-up windows or empty buildings remind me how quickly life changes and how we forget the lifestyles and values of a generation before.

Before Ron's dad passed away, he spoke to each of the children and grandchildren privately, telling them the last words he wanted to leave with them. It was a powerful experience to pass on the sentiments and advice you don't want left unsaid. One thing I remember him saying is that it takes just one generation to remove a heritage of faith. That stuck with me.

We have a stewardship responsibility to be mindful of how our actions affect the future of those around us. There's a saying that as the leader goes, so goes the nation. Our societal idol of living in the moment affects our children, grandchildren, the environment, and our circle of influence. When we don't consider the consequences of our actions and choices on future generations, we tend to leave a legacy of destruction. Our collective lack of foresight due to immediate gratification and selfish ambition has created a culture of addiction, violence, racism, and environmental disaster that is handed down like the prized family photo album.

We have a choice about the heirlooms and legacies we leave. We can leave footprints to follow or wounds to heal.[1] This is a reminder of foresight's importance. We want insight for today and foresight for tomorrow, so we're not left with hindsight of regret. We can develop these wise perspectives by creating a new mindset to see beyond today.

A NEW MINDSET

We often don't engage foresight until something prompts us to question something we have taken for granted. As a parent, I didn't think much about expectations for household chore responsibilities until my oldest son came of age to do the tasks his older sister did, like laundry or unloading the dishwasher. In that moment foresight made me pause.

I grew up with all sisters and we each had the same household chores—I had never thought about different chore expectations among sons or daughters. I realized that excusing our sons from more traditional housekeeping tasks could create unintentional expectations for future spouses to fulfill traditional gender roles. It was a defining moment as a parent, helping me develop a mindset for how my expectations can influence my children's future beliefs. (In case you wonder, we created an equal-opportunity household.)

A foresight mindset prompts us to evaluate how our habits, beliefs, and practices intentionally or unintentionally affect others. A simple mindset shift can make a positive difference to those around you. If you are a parent or grandparent, your children and grandchildren absorb and internalize your words and behaviors. Thinking of your influence this way, you may refrain from certain behaviors when your kids are at home or be more intentional about changing unhealthy habits.

While it takes one generation to abandon one facet of heritage, it also only takes one person to make a better life for future generations. Our choices to foster a healthy heritage or stop an unhealthy one are powerful. I think of how my grandma's foresight to save money for home ownership gave my dad a better life. In turn, it influenced his priorities for my sisters and me.

THE GIFT GOES ON

My dad prioritized a college education for his children because of his upbringing; his parents left their country and family for a better life for him. His hard work and commitment to helping us obtain degrees helped me value the opportunity for higher education. It has influenced me as an educator to ensure all students know that meaningful career and college options are within their reach.

Several years ago, a former student told me she had just finished her master's degree. She thanked me for believing in her college dream when others discouraged her. I was unaware

I had done so at the time. But somehow my words had helped inspire her, and she ended up putting herself through school and graduated with honors.

Though unintended, my grandmother's foresight to better her family's position was a legacy she left behind for many, not just her children and grandchildren. Your legacy may be different, but it is just as critical. Your special *something* impacts your circle and ripples out to others. One family I know values entrepreneurship, ingenuity, and hard work. They have built a legacy of business enterprises that inspires others. When each of us follows the path God sets before us, we leave a legacy beyond ourselves.

SCRIPTURE APPLICATION

Could it be that God foresees the heritage and legacy he desires us to live out and leave behind? I think that's the core of the soul seed he plants in us so young. He is the author of our past, present, and future; when we pause and listen to the Holy Spirit, we can better discern how he's orchestrating things we cannot currently see. As Isaiah 30:21 says, "Whether you turn to the right or to the left, your ears will hear a voice behind you, saying, 'This is the way; walk in it.'" When we walk on God's path, we are creating the life he has imagined for us that will be passed down as an inheritance to our children (Proverbs 13:22).

What we pass down to our children isn't just the substance of our lives; it is a witness to God when we remember God's faithfulness to us. Deuteronomy 32 calls the Israelites to not only remember God, but to remember who they are: "Remember the days of old; consider the generations of long past," says Deuteronomy 32:7. We create a living spiritual legacy by sharing our life lessons and speaking of God's faithfulness. This glorifies God and connects children, grandchildren, and those we influence with the gospel of Christ. Inside that soul seed is not just our dream or calling that God puts in us; it is also the greatest calling for all humankind.

In Ecclesiastes 3:11, we read that God sets eternity in our hearts. This longing for the God of eternity leads us to search for *that something* of fulfillment, restoration, and hope beyond humanity. God reconciled a broken relationship with us and provided a heritage of eternal life through the death and resurrection of his son, Jesus Christ. *This is the way; walk in it* is the invitation to join him.

We invite others, including our children, to know about Jesus through rhythmic faith practices—such as attending church, praying at mealtime, reading Bible stories at bedtime, or memorizing scripture. One friend told me recently how Bible verses she memorized in a scripture memory program as a child got her through a difficult season. Someone's faithfulness to teach her those verses left a legacy in her life.

Yet what matters even more for a spiritual heritage is authentic faith lived out. This happens when our lifestyle aligns with our priorities. We live what we believe, and that is what we leave behind.

MAKING FORESIGHT A LIFESTYLE

A legacy lifestyle, like you see among the Amish, starts with simple practices based on your values. When our kids were young, we valued the practice of intentionally connecting once a week. With a larger family, I wanted to leave a heritage of interconnectedness. I also wanted to pass on a legacy of faith, modeling a lifestyle connected to God and lived out amongst each other.

Every Sunday evening, we gathered, read Scripture, and shared about our week. Then we prayed. It was not idyllic. Most often, it was awkward. But as the years unfolded, the time we spent praying for and listening to one another overshadowed the eye rolls and interruptions. It set a practice and tradition that lasted until the last one left for college.

In the aftermath of Ron's accident, foresight caused me to wonder how we could still gather consistently as a family, despite being hundreds of miles apart. Life had changed almost instantaneously. How could we still foster a heritage of faith and connection?

We have created a simple new tradition. On Sunday evenings, Ron starts a group text where each of us shares our week's highlight and an upcoming prayer request. It allows each adult in our family to engage according to their availability and comfort level, sharing what they want their parents and siblings to know. Ron and I pray over those requests. It stewards a family legacy despite distance and changing lives. I hope it plants seeds for the next generation.

This is just one simple practice that, with foresight, creates a family heritage we hope will continue. How would you like to implement your values into your lifestyle? The place to start is not adding more activities but letting go of what creates an unwanted legacy of busyness.

LET GO OF BUSYNESS

Living an heirloom life is within everyone's reach. It doesn't require a picture-perfect farmhouse you can pass down to your children. It does require uncomplicating your life from unimportant things that zap your time and energy. Such activities leave you with little to show for your efforts—both now and certainly in the future.

Most of this is summed up in the phrase *being busy*. Busyness is filling your time with a haphazard frenzy of unimportant tasks without knowing why you are doing them. Busyness is often driven by striving, avoiding, or pacifying expectations or hurt. It crowds out the pauses of prudence and foresight and robs you of a legacy-filled life.

For years, I thought busyness meant being admirably productive, like that Proverbs 31 superwoman. Trying to meet idealistic expectations of being the perfect wife, mom, teacher, and Christian left me stressed out and burned out instead. I took my irritation and negative reactions out on my family. I wasn't living the legacy I wanted to leave. I pivoted by letting go of what complicated the life I wanted by changing careers, healing wounds, and creating a healthier lifestyle.

Children at school often tell me their parents are too busy to help or listen to them. When a child says that, it really means they are unsure whether a parent sees them or is willing to make time for them. My kids were the same. When my son Ethan was in sixth grade, he created a board game at school for an assignment. One night, I was writing an article on my computer when he asked me if I was busy while holding the board game in his hands.

I wanted to say yes—I was on a deadline and I don't like playing board games. But I knew he was asking me if I would enter his world and marvel at what he made. We sat together on the floor, and in ten minutes, we completed the game. Afterward, I went back to my writing, and I noticed that he had the biggest smile. I have learned that if someone, especially a loved one, asks if you're busy, they are really inquiring if you have time for them.

An heirloom life means letting go of busy task-doing and replacing it with time generously given to the most important people and commitments for your life stage. It means having a schedule that pauses for what's most important. In various moments or life stages, that might be people, rest, nature, God, or many other activities. Life never slows unless we intentionally decelerate, pausing to enjoy life's journey.

REGULAR RHYTHMS

These rhythmic pauses look different depending on your lifestyle or needs. When my kids were home, I often took a day or afternoon away from home for reflection and recalibration when a full season was ahead. Time alone helped me manage the hustle and bustle of family life. It also made me less irritable and more willing to deal with disruptions and disappointments.

I have also learned to balance busyness by simply committing to not doing it all. This means delegating tasks, rightsizing my life, and making space for rest, play, and healthy processes. I've often prioritized sessions with counselors or mentors who can help me with different needs, personally and professionally. I've passed on church responsibilities or speaking opportunities when my kids needed me more at home. Sometimes, I even have to say no to loved ones, which I often did while writing this book. Accepting life's *both/and* tensions also reduces stress by diminishing unrealistic expectations.

Finally, your priorities are greatly refined by nurturing your relationship with Jesus through consistent prayer, Bible reading, and spiritual reflection. The Holy Spirit cultivates what only he can—love, joy, peace, patience, kindness, goodness, gentleness, faithfulness, and self-control. These qualities, above all, cultivate the heritage and legacy you desire.

CULTIVATING HERITAGE AND LEGACY

When I became a grandma a short time ago, I realized *this was it!* Life never presents itself twice. I no longer have the luxury of looking to the future. It has arrived. Soul seeds won't bloom on our deathbeds. There's only one time for what's most important. That time is now.

Since childhood, I dreamed of passing meaningful things down to my children and grandchildren. I imagined writing a story about our ancestors' life experiences. I pictured being a retired grandma with time on my hands, making a quilt with material and clothes I've kept in the cedar chest for decades.

Foresight has made me pause as a new grandma, realizing tangible heirlooms don't create themselves. When our first grandchild was born during the pandemic, I started cutting and piecing material from clothing and other items that belonged to our son, to Ron and me, to our parents and grandparents. Bob and Grandpa's flannel shirts, my dad's plaid dress shirt, Lois's jeans, my Italian grandma's handmade curtains—each cloth was a physical connection to people, now gone, who impacted my life.

I took one step at a time until a hand-pieced quilt was bound in a quilt frame, ready to stitch. I'm not a seamstress or an experienced quilter—just a woman with a soul seed and resourcefulness to create a heritage for the next generation.

Two years later, upon signing the contract for *Uncompli-cated*, the quilt still sat untouched in the frame. Life got busier after the pandemic and responsibilities crowded out such a project. Several more hours were needed to complete it. Prudence said *git-r-done*. With one more grandchild born and one on the way, my soul seed answered, "I will."

The process of completing the quilt was a convergence of the past, present, and future all in one place. As I finished the stitches, remembering the lessons learned from each person's impact on my life, I touched *that something*. It was an emotional, sacred space where I dwelled for several days, feeling the tangible presence of God's goodness in my life.

I also realized only I would know who these people were if I didn't pass their stories down to the next generation. I made a quick booklet through Canva with photos and a brief narrative telling my grandson Luca to whom each cloth belonged and their relationship to him. It didn't take long, but it was worth the effort I put into it.

Late into the night, finishing things up, God showed me the beautiful tapestry of the life he unfolds for each of us. God has such a tapestry for you, too. Though the quilt encompasses my heritage, it's a tangible representation for all of us. You have your own customs, traditions, and memory markers of the lives that influence you. Whatever those artifacts are, they remind us that stories, people, and experiences make a difference in our circles of influence.

Could the simple secrets to a vibrant life be nothing more than living the life we are given? Our life is a gift and is the legacy we leave behind. A beautiful, uncomplicated, and compelling life.

> Let Your work appear to Your servants,
> And Your glory to their children.
> And let the beauty of the LORD our God be upon us,
> And establish the work of our hands for us;
> Yes, establish the work of our hands.
> —Psalm 90:16–17 (NKJV)

SIMPLE SECRETS: NEXT STEPS

Now it's your turn. Here are simple suggestions to practice foresight, heritage, and legacy and uncomplicate your life.

- Revive a passion or interest you would like to grow. Perhaps you could write poetry, crochet, volunteer, or do something you have put off in this season.

- Create a heritage drawer or closet where you keep items you may want to use for a craft or future project.
- Make a scrapbook for your children or take special trips with them.
- Write down lessons you have learned from your experiences or others. Share them with your children or grandchildren, or write a book about them!
- Start a new tradition with your family or revive an old one, sharing its meaning or cultural significance.
- Research traditions of your family's cultural heritage. Choose one to incorporate into your life.
- Make an appointment to steward your mental, emotional, or spiritual wellness. It could be a massage appointment, counseling, or a new mentor relationship.
- Consider your priorities: Are you busy or living a full life? Take steps to remove unintentional busyness toward a full, but not too full, life.
- Practice reflective prayers, talking to God but taking a moment to pause, listen, and reflect. Perhaps journal, draw, or garden while listening.
- Make a timeline of significant spiritual or personal milestones in your life.

Prayer pause: *Invite Jesus to reveal what he desires for you from this chapter.*

REFLECTION

1. In a simple sentence, what legacy would you like to leave behind? Plan three next steps for how to create this reality.
2. Who in your life exemplified foresight? What would you like to model from their life?

3. What did you learn from this chapter that is most helpful, or what reflects your needs and hopes? How will you apply this to your life?
4. What is one lesson of foresight from your life that you can retell to another person?

Conclusion

The LORD will watch over your coming and going both now and forevermore.
—Psalm 121:8

Sandy, my spiritual director, listened to me describe the content of *Uncomplicated* and was curious about the tears streaming down my face. I told her that writing this book, with stories and experiences of mine and others, was like coming back to *that something* I longed to live—and in hindsight I realized I had. Putting words to how these ten secrets have positively shaped and impacted my life settled me.

"It's like a homecoming," she said, mirroring what she heard me say. Yes, a homecoming was an image that resonated in my soul.

I hope *Uncomplicated: Simple Secrets for a Compelling Life* is like a homecoming for you also. I pray it shows you that the soul seeds and *that something* you long for isn't in a place you visit, like Amish country, or an unattainable lifestyle, or from a distant memory. Instead, these timeless secrets are transferable and relevant today—and desperately needed in every pocket of modern culture. As the world moves swiftly toward artificial intelligence, and political and cultural chaos, your uncomplicated, compelling life will immediately influence the lives of those around you like those whose stories in this book have impacted mine.

Let's revisit the importance of each of the ten secrets and how they invite us to come home to an uncomplicated life:

- *Contentment:* Rather than looking for *that something* you long for that will make you happy in a person, place, or experience, God invites you, through contentment, to thrive in the beautiful life he has created for you.
- *Resourcefulness:* Your newfound ability to creatively cope with difficult situations or unusual problems will eliminate anxiety and help you overcome daily obstacles and big life disruptions.
- *Prudence:* You have learned how to shed impulsivity and excessiveness by making wise decisions regarding finances, relationships, and personal choices.
- *Practicality:* Your ability to manage time, relationships, and resources with practical, sustainable tools will simplify all areas of your life.
- *Fidelity:* You are able to determine who and what is most important and how to uncomplicate your life by being loyal to the people and values most important to you.
- *Forbearance and equanimity:* You have learned strategies to regulate emotions, and have a calm, balanced approach to life's difficulties rather than reacting or overreacting.
- *Stewardship:* You have learned how to tend to those entrusted to your care, making your life a protective shield to those around you, including how to care for yourself.
- *Interdependence:* You have learned how to engage reciprocity, vulnerability, and interdependent relationships

with people, nature, and God, and you value the richness it adds to your life and others.

- *Groundedness and humility:* You are able to create a more authentic life that makes you more comfortable with yourself and others—your presence being a calming gift to those you are with.
- *Foresight, heritage, and legacy:* You have learned how to think beyond today to create the kind of imprint you desire to leave upon your spheres of influence, both now and in the future.

My prayer is that *Uncomplicated* will be like the books I have often returned to over the years—*The Memories of Hoosier Homemakers* series and Elisabeth Elliot's *Keep a Quiet Heart.*[1] These books ground me in my core values and remind me how to live them out in a world where they are modeled less and less. I also hope *Uncomplicated* models how to foster *that something* God wants to grow in your own life.

I pray that within these pages, something calls you back home to what is most important. I hope you'll take a few prompts from the *Simple Secrets: Next Steps* section in each chapter to walk it out in your life. I hope you will reflect on the questions, or discuss them with a group of friends, recalling and utilizing your own stories and lessons.

Finally, I'd love to hear how *Uncomplicated* has impacted your life, even just the slightest bit. Feel free to email me at brenda@brendayoder.com with your stories of how this book has prompted a less complicated but compelling life for you. Each story you share will be a homecoming for both of us, and the secrets lived out will create an uncomplicated, compelling life that is a legacy lifestyle you leave behind.

Acknowledgments

It's challenging to give adequate credit to an entire community or the dozens of people who have influenced my life or lifestyle. But I want to acknowledge my church family and the broader community for *that something* that isn't perfect but is an incredible heritage and legacy.

I want to acknowledge the Yoder family, including Catherine. We have the most incredible legacy and heritage of *that something* that started with Bob and Lois.

My husband Ron—thank you for sharing our life in this book.

Thanks to the mastermind group for the first head nods for this book. Further thanks to Ann Kroeker, writing coach, who brought this idea to life. Also to Bob Hostetler, my agent, and the Herald Press staff for bringing this to reality: Amy, Laura, and Elisabeth!

Thanks to Sarah Forgrave, Amelia Rhodes, and my Stonecroft sisters who prayed me through this project. To the significant women who are embedded on these pages: Naomi, Donna, Alli, Andrea, Ingrid, Amy, Laura, Jamelle, Tami, Marian, Lou Anne, Kala, and Erin. To Kris, Joanna, Linda, and Heidi—your family emulates this type of life. Also to my former and current students, from whom I continally learn.

Thank you to my children and their spouses, our grandchildren, and the next generation whose lives are also embedded in this book. Thank you for the legacy of influence you're already leaving. I'm incredibly proud to be your mom and Mimi.

To my mom and sisters and sisters-in-law who lead such beautiful and compelling lives.

Finally, to those who have left behind an incredible legacy on my life and others—particularly Deb, Ervin, Dad, Bob, and Lois.

Notes

INTRODUCTION

1. Kevin D. Miller, "Technological Prudence: What the Amish Can Teach Us," Center for Christian Ethics at Baylor University, 2011, 20–28, https://www.baylor.edu/content/services/document.php/130953.pdf.

2. Quote attributed to Brian Brett, accessed September 2, 2023, from *AZ Quotes*, https://www.azquotes.com/quote/787182, which references Brian Brett, *Trauma Farm: A Rebel History of Rural Life* (Vancouver, BC: Greystone Books Ltd, 2009), 16.

3. Eleanor Arnold, ed., *Living Rich Lives Vol. 6, Memories of Hoosier Homemakers Series* (Bloomington, IN: Indiana University Press, 1990), 234.

4. "Partners in Life Skills Education: Conclusions from a United Nations Inter-Agency Meeting," Department of Mental Health, Social Change and Mental Health Cluster, World Health Organization, 1999, https://www.orientamentoirreer.it/sites/default/files/materiali/1999%20OMS%20lifeskills%20edizione%201999.pdf.

CHAPTER 1: CONTENTMENT

1. Quote attributed to Alfred Nobel, *Brainy Quotes*, accessed September 2, 2023, https://www.brainyquote.com/quotes/alfred_nobel_556206.

2. Eleanor Arnold, ed., *Living Rich Lives Vol. 6, Memories of Hoosier Homemakers Series* (Bloomington, IN: Indiana University Press, 1990), 234.

3. Jenn Williamson, "All Sufficient Grace," *Thrive Global Women*, April 21, 2020, https://thriveconnection.com/2020/04/21/all-sufficient-grace/, originally posted at *Four for France* (blog), January 14, 2015.

4. Arnold, *Living Rich Lives*, 229.

CHAPTER 2: RESOURCEFULNESS

1. Elisabeth Elliot, "Doing the Next Thing," originally presented at the Billy Graham Training Center, Asheville, NC, November 6–8, 1992. I heard Elisabeth Elliot cite this principle on various occasions throughout my life on her *Gateway to Joy* radio program. This principle is explained in this lecture, third in a series, *Waiting on God*, which can be accessed on YouTube at https://youtu.be/Nt6ATqaik5g?si=c9DJoMZWdAAdO77B, copyright by the Elisabeth Elliot Foundation.

2. Eleanor Arnold, ed., *Living Rich Lives Vol. 6, Memories of Hoosier Homemakers Series* (Bloomington, IN: Indiana University Press, 1990), 86.

3. Quote attributed to Franklin D. Roosevelt, *Brainy Quotes*, accessed July 23, 2023, https://www.brainyquote.com/quotes/franklin_d_roosevelt_101840.

4. Jay Desko, "7 Lies Every Leader Needs to Stop Believing Today," *The Center Consulting Group* (blog), January 31, 2023, https://www.centerconsulting.org/ blog/7-lies-every-leader-needs-to-stop-believing-today, quoting Jonathan Haidt and Greg Lukianoff, *The Coddling of the American Mind* (London: Penguin Publishing Group, 2019).

5. "What Are Anxiety Disorders?," American Psychiatric Association, accessed July 19, 2023, https://www.psychiatry.org/patients-families/anxiety-disorders/what-are-anxiety-disorders.

6. Arnold, *Living Rich Lives*, 231.

7. Brother Lawrence and Marshall Davis, *The Practice of the Presence of God in Modern English* (Independently published, 2013), 22.

CHAPTER 3: PRUDENCE

1. Quote attributed to Jeremy Collier, English theologian, *Forbes*, accessed July 12, 2023, https://www.forbes.com/quotes/author/jeremy-collier/.

2. Kevin D. Miller, "Technological Prudence: What the Amish Can Teach Us," Center for Christian Ethics at Baylor University, 2011, 25.

3. Miller, 25.

4. Miller, 26.

5. Eleanor Arnold, ed., *Living Rich Lives Vol. 6, Memories of Hoosier Homemakers Series* (Bloomington, IN: Indiana University Press, 1990), 21.

CHAPTER 4: PRACTICALITY

1. Quote attributed to Paul Engle, *Brainy Quotes*, accessed July 24, 2023, https://www. brainyquote.com/authors/paul-engle-quotes.

2. Cited in Susan Milligan and Laura Camera, "Ditch the Degree? Many Employers Are Just Fine with That," *U.S. News and World Report*, February 3, 2023, https://www. usnews.com/news/the-report/articles/2023-02-03/ditch-the-degree-many-employers-are-just-fine-with-that.

3. The Real Deal of Parenting (@realdealofparentingofficial), quote by Cheyenne, Life Skills for Kids (@farmhousebookco), "We don't need productivity advice from 23-year-old boss babes. We need productivity tips from our great-grandmothers. These ladies juggled milking cows, baking bread, raising 12 kids all while managing to quilt a few cushions. Like ma'am . . . how?," *Instagram*, February 2, 2023, https://www. instagram.com/p/CoKfmTlr_wq/?hl=en.

4. Wikipedia, citing Roger Steer, *George Müller: Delighted in God* (Tain, UK: Christian Focus, 1997), 131, https://en.wikipedia.org/wiki/George_Müller.

5. L. B. Cowman, *Streams in the Desert* (Grand Rapids, MI: Zondervan, 1996), 157.

CHAPTER 5: FIDELITY

1. Quote attributed to Mother Teresa, quoted by Dr. Mary C. McDonald, "Called to Faithfulness, Not Success," *Memphis Daily News*, June 22, 2017, accessed July 17, 2023, https://www.memphisdailynews.com/news/2017/jun/22/called-to-faithfulness-not-success/.

2. "Patient Dog Waits for Days Outside Hospital," *The Guardian*, January 21, 2021, https://www.theguardian.com/world/2021/jan/22/patient-dog-waits-for-days-outside-hospital.

3. Quote attributed to Stephen Covey, *AZ Quotes*, accessed September 3, 2023, cited from *The 7 Habits of Highly Effective People: Powerful Lessons in Personal Change Interactive Edition* (Coral Gables, FL: Mango Media Inc., 2016), 241, https://www.azquotes.com/quote/588123.

4. Jeffrey M. Jones, "Is Marriage Becoming Irrelevant?," *Gallup News*, December 28, 2020, https://news.gallup.com/poll/316223/fewer-say-important-parents-married.aspx.

5. Jon J. Muth, *The Three Questions* (New York: Scholastic Press, 2002).

CHAPTER 6: FORBEARANCE AND EQUANIMITY

1. Quote attributed to Eleanor Roosevelt, *AZ Quotes*, accessed September 2, 2023, https://www.azquotes.com/quote/462346.

CHAPTER 7: STEWARDSHIP

1. I originally found this poem handwritten by Lois Yoder, entitled "My Daily Prayer." An internet search attributes this poem to Grenville Kleiser, with only a few citations. "My Daily Prayer," *AGP Poems—The Only Way* (blog), accessed July 25, 2023, http://www.agp-internet.com/react/poems/00000096fe1134a0a/000000975d0dd6601.html.

2. *Confession of Faith in a Mennonite Perspective* (Scottdale, PA: Herald Press, 1995).

3. Quote attributed to Bob Goff, obtained from *AZ Quotes*, accessed July 25, 2023, https://www.azquotes.com/quote/813608, which attributes original citation from a Bob Goff Facebook post, May 28, 2014, https://www.facebook.com/bobgoffis/posts/651762941565649.

4. Quote attributed to Audrey Hepburn, *AZ Quotes*, accessed September 3, 2023, https://www.azquotes.com/quote/1399235.

5. Jonathan Haidt, "Social Media Is a Major Cause of the Mental Illness Epidemic in Teen Girls. Here's the Evidence," *After Babel* (blog), February 22, 2023, https://jonathanhaidt.substack.com/p/social-media-mental-illness-epidemic.

6. Viktor E. Frankl, *Yes to Life: In Spite of Everything* (Boston: Beacon Press, 2019), 36.

7. Kleiser, "My Daily Prayer."

8. Laura van Dernoot Lipsky and Connie Burk, *Trauma Stewardship: An Everyday Guide to Caring for Self While Caring for Others* (Berrett-Koehler Publishers, 2009). Includes many principles helpful to steward secondary trauma, including some from other faith practices.

CHAPTER 8: INTERDEPENDENCE

1. Quote attributed to Thomas Merton, *AZ Quotes*, accessed July 14, 2023, https://www.azquotes.com/quote/536914.

2. Richard Louv, *Last Child in the Woods: Saving Our Children from Nature-Deficit Disorder* (Chapel Hill, NC: Algonquin Books, 2008).

3. Danielle Cohen, "Why Kids Need to Spend Time in Nature," Child Mind Institute, April 14, 2023, https://childmind.org/article/why-kids-need-to-spend-time-in-nature/.

4. Amity Hook-Sopko, "Kids Who Spend More Time in Nature Become Happier Adults, Study Confirms," *Green Child Magazine*, April 26, 2021, https://www.greenchildmagazine.com/kids-who-spend-more-time-in-nature-become-happier-adults/, cites study by Kristine Engemann, Carsten Bocker Pedersen, Lars Arge, and Jens-Christian Svenning, "Residential Green Space in Childhood is Associated with Lower Risk of Psychiatric Disorders from Adolescence into Adulthood," PNAS, February 25, 2019, https://www.pnas.org/doi/10.1073/pnas.1807504116.

5. Eleanor Arnold, ed., *Girlhood Days Vol. 4, Memories of Hoosier Homemakers Series* (Bloomington, IN: Indiana University Press, 1990), 19.

CHAPTER 9: GROUNDEDNESS AND HUMILITY

1. "A Farmer's Humility," *Earth Haven Farm* (blog), accessed July 20, 2023, cited Catherine de Hueck Doherty, *Apostolic Farming, Healing the Earth* (Combermere, ON: Madonna House, 1991), https://earthhaven.ca/blog/a-farmers-humility/156.

2. Jill Savage's books, *No More Perfect Moms*, *No More Perfect Kids*, and *No More Perfect Marriages* (all Chicago: Moody Press), and *The No More Perfect Podcast* can be found at jillsavage.org.

3. "Polarization Greatest Threat to U.S. Right Now, Former Defense Secretary Says," *Face the Nation*, YouTube Short, https://youtu.be/aMrBV9iRCiQ, accessed July 20, 2023, citing Margaret Brennan's full interview, "Interview with Former Defense Secretary," on *Face the Nation*, May 21, 2023, CBS, https://www.cbsnews.com/video/full-interview-former-defense-secretary-robert-gates-on-face-the-nation-may-21-2023/.

4. Brooke Meredith, "Kindness and Humility Have Taken a Nosedive in America," Medium, December 29, 2019, https://medium.com/swlh/kindness-and-humility-have-taken-a-nosedive-in-america-67a1d912d53c.

CHAPTER 10: FORESIGHT, HERITAGE, AND LEGACY

1. A life principle attributed to Gerry Brooksprin (@gerrybrooksprin) Instagram reel, October 11, 2023, https://www.instagram.com/p/CyRsWVrtW41/.

CONCLUSION

1. Elisabeth Elliot, *Keep a Quiet Heart* (Ann Arbor, MI: Vine Books, 1995).

The Author

Brenda L. Yoder, LMHC, is a counselor, speaker, author, and educator. She is the author of *Fledge: Launching Your Kids Without Losing Your Mind* and cohost of the *Midlife Moms Podcast* and Facebook group. She also hosts and writes the *Life Beyond the Picket Fence* podcast and blog, covering a variety of topics on faith, life, and family beyond the  storybook image. Brenda is currently a part-time elementary counselor and therapist in private practice. She and her husband, Ron, are parents to four adult children and two daughters-in-law, and grandparents to three grandsons with whom they love creating new memories. Brenda and Ron live on a farm in Shipshewana, Indiana, where she loves gardening and spending evenings sitting in her front porch rocker.